RUN
RHINO
RUN

RUN RHINO RUN

Esmond and Chryssee Bradley Martin

With an Introduction by **Elspeth Huxley**
Photographs by **Mohamed Amin**

1982
CHATTO & WINDUS
LONDON

This book is dedicated to our families.

First published 1982 by
Chatto & Windus Ltd
40 William IV Street
London WC2N 4DF

British Library Cataloguing in Publication Data
Martin, Esmond Bradley
   Run, rhino, run.
   1. Rhinoceroses
   I. Title   II. Martin, Chryssee Bradley
   III. Amin, Mohamed
   599.72'8   QL737.U63
ISBN 0-7011-2632-9

© Camerapix 1982
This book was designed and produced by
Camerapix Publishers International,
P.O. Box 45048,
Nairobi, Kenya

Phototypeset by Keyspools Ltd, Golborne, Lancs
Printed in Italy by Arnoldo Mondadori, Verona

Contents

Acknowledgements

From the day I decided to study rhinos, it was only a matter of time before I became interested in the uses of rhino products and the ways in which they are traded. I was most fortunate that the World Wildlife Fund and the International Union for Conservation of Nature and Natural Resources were also very concerned about the fate of the rhino and endorsed my proposals to carry out research on this trade. The World Wildlife Fund and IUCN sponsored several of my trips overseas, and much of what I learnt abroad is included in these pages. I wish to thank these two international conservation agencies for their support.

My research led me across continents and to some places I had never previously visited. I found scholars, traders, shopkeepers, conservationists and medical practitioners more than willing to assist me in my quest to learn why the various parts of the rhino's anatomy, gram for gram, are so valuable on the world market today. Their help was invaluable, and I certainly could not have written this book without their co-operation. I am most grateful to all those who gave of their time and knowledge so generously to me. I would also like to note a very special thanks to Ian Parker for the help he gave to me right from the beginning of my research. He took particular interest in it, gave me 'clues' to several mysteries about the rhino trade, and kindly offered constructive comments during the preparation of my manuscript.

Below, I list the names of many other people who have contributed in innumerable ways to this study of rhinos, for which I am most appreciative:

In Europe and America: Peter Beard, Michael Birch, Thom Friedlein, Andrew Laurie, Pierre Portas, Peter Sand, Wilfred Thesiger, Russell Train, Douglas J. K. Wright and the administrative officers of the World Wildlife Fund and the International Union for Conservation of Nature and Natural Resources.

In Africa: George Adamson, Jeremy Anderson, Hermann Bentley, Markus Borner, Sonia Boyle, Ina and Colin Britz, Martin Brooks, D. H. Cumming, Heini Demmer, Rodney Elliott, Ted Goss, Ian Grimwood, Anthony Hall-Martin, Kes Hillman, Peter Hitchins, Colin Hugo, Brian Huntley, John Ilsley, Peter Jenkins, Peter Joffe, John King, Norman Miller, E. T. Monks, K. M. Naidoo, Mike Norton-Griffiths, Norman Owen-Smith, Chris Parker, Ian Player, Pixie Ross, T. C. I. Ryan, Daphne Sheldrick, Clive Spinage, Steve Stephenson, B. R. Stevens, Brian Tring, John Varty, P. J. Viljoen, John Vincent, Clive Walker, David Western, John White and Bill Woodley.

In Asia: M. N. Adhikary, Selma Al-Radi, A. Bose, Na Chih-Liang, Doyle Damman, A. K. Das, Shahi Hakim, Chris Huxley, Toshio Ito, H. T. Jun, J. W. Jun, P. C. Kalita, Sung-Keel Kang, P. Kannan, Lee Suk Kyu, Boonsong Lekagul, Pong Leng-Ee, Kojiro Mino, H. M. Mohsin, Uhla Myint, Cynthia Myntti, Y. Nagai, Dominic Ng, Sayagyi U Nyunt, G. N. Pant, K. R. S. Proud, B. K. Bardhan Roy, M. A. Partha Sarathy, Dalbir Singh, R. N. Sonowal, Nico van Strien, Stephen Lau Kiew Teck, M. V. Wani and E. Yanagida.

NOTE TO THE READER

My wife, Chryssee, and I collaborated on the research for this book. Together we have written the text. However, for the sake of clarity and for simplicity of style, we decided to use throughout the first person singular (referring to myself). We also hope that in writing this way we will be able to achieve more immediacy.

December 1981   *Esmond Bradley Martin*

Introduction

The 1970s may have been a good period for many in our consumer society, but for the rhinoceros it was a decade of disaster. In those ten years, 50 per cent of the world's rhino population disappeared.

The black rhino bore the brunt of the damage. In eastern Africa, formerly the stronghold of the species, nine out of ten of these cumbrous, vulnerable and endearing creatures were wiped out. Most of the killing was done by poachers carrying out their cruel trade to meet the demand for rhino horn in Asia and the Middle East.

In the mid 1940s, a single hunter shot just under 1,000 rhinos in an area of 200 square kilometres in eastern Kenya, to make way for African settlement. By 1980, an area 100 times as large, the adjoining Tsavo National Park, held only about 150 surviving rhinos. An animal that has inhabited the earth for some 60 million years is now reduced to a few thousands that cling onto survival in little pockets of bush and jungle set aside for their protection. And even there they are being relentlessly hunted, trapped and killed.

Despite much discussion, argument and wringing of hands, despite expressions of concern by governments, despite efforts by dedicated individuals to halt the trend towards extinction, the remarkable truth is that no investigation into the demand for rhino horn, the root cause of the trouble, was made until 1979. Then Dr Esmond Bradley Martin, sponsored by the World Wildlife Fund, travelled through much of South-East Asia in order to find out who buys the horn, in what quantities, and for what purposes. He discovered that some of the most widespread preconceptions about the trade were wrong. That rhino horn was used in aphrodisiac concoctions, in the mistaken belief that it increased sexual virility, was the generally accepted doctrine. By questioning the people who actually sold the horn, the pharmacists—nearly all Chinese—of Singapore, Hong Kong, Macao, Taipei and elsewhere, Dr Martin found out that its main use is not as an aphrodisiac after all, but as a remedy for various ailments such as high fevers, headaches, arthritis and other infirmities. In parts of India it is indeed believed to stimulate sexual performance, but throughout South-East Asia, as well as in China, it forms part of traditional Chinese medicine practiced today, much as it was 1,000 years ago, alongside modern treatments using scientifically based drugs.

From the rhino's point of view, of course, it does not really matter whether the protuberance on its nose is believed to be an aphrodisiac or a cure for fevers; in either case, the persecution of the species by the human race stems from a myth. But it is as well to establish the facts before seeking a remedy.

Dr Martin also tells us that another market hungry for the horn lies in North Yemen, where daggers with elaborately carved rhino horn handles are highly prized by young men. Until recently, very few young men could afford them, but a seven-fold rise in per capita income has put them within the reach of almost everyone. The new wealth has so greatly increased the demand that this small country, with about six million inhabitants, has become the world's largest importer of the horn—an unexpected and, for the rhino, melancholy spin-off from the soaring price of oil.

Trade in rhino products is banned by CITES—the Convention on International Trade in Endangered Species—and so every country which has ratified this agreement, and which still imports or exports the horn, does so illegally. Nevertheless a thriving trade goes on, with a host of agents, smugglers, wholesalers, retailers and financiers involved in a loosely linked but highly effective network stretching from the Chinese pharmacist in, say, Singapore or Taipei, to the national park employee in India or Africa who may be underpaid, inadequately supervised and ill-equipped and so, not surprisingly, an easy target for bribery or intimidation. When one considers that a single horn of an Indian rhino may be worth the equivalent of three years' wages as a farm labourer or hotel waiter, the prevalence of bribery and smuggling is understandable.

Altogether it is a gloomy picture for all five existing species of rhino. The Javan species is down to an estimated 50 individuals clinging to existence in a small reserve at the western tip of that island. Probably no more than 300 of the Sumatran race exist in very small and scattered populations. The Indian species is rather better off; a population of about 1,500 dwells in national parks in India and Nepal, and vigorous measures are being taken by those governments to protect them. The one real success story concerns the white, or square-lipped, rhino of southern Africa. Hunted to the very verge of extinction, it was rescued by the Natal park authorities and, under protection, has built up its numbers to a point where populations have been established in other parts of Africa, as well as in many zoos. It is the black rhino that has been really hard hit. For any animal, there is a point of no return when numbers have so fallen that the likelihood of males and females encountering each other in the bush is virtually nil. This point has now been reached in many parts of a habitat that formerly covered most of Africa south of the Sahara.

Conservationists will tend to focus their attention on Dr Martin's final chapter, "Prospects for Rhinos". While the outlook is certainly grim, he does not think it hopeless, except possibly for the Javan and Sumatran species. Better policing and management of national parks is the first priority. It is easy enough to say this, exceedingly difficult to bring it about. As Dr Martin points out, the breakdown of law and order is a factor which no amount of support from wildlife organizations and international bodies can remedy. In Uganda, parks built up for decades to a high level of excellence, and major magnets for a lucrative tourist trade, have been utterly shattered. The animals have been slaughtered wholesale, first by Idi Amin's undisciplined soldiery, then by Tanzanian soldiers equally out of control, and by virtually anyone with a rifle who wanted a meal. In other parts of Africa as well, guerrilla warfare has made nonsense of measures to protect wild animals, and the animals have died.

Nevertheless, in most African countries the parks are being maintained, if not always with efficiency, because their value to the tourist industry is recognized. What is mainly needed is more money. There is also a need for better techniques. International wildlife bodies are often willing to supply Land Rovers, light aircraft and other forms of modern equipment, but Dr Martin believes that these may be less effective than old-fashioned foot patrols which, giving no noisy warning of their approach, can track down poachers more effectively. Not only must anti-poaching measures be stepped up and greatly improved, but penalties need to be made much more severe, and the law more honestly enforced. "The deterrent has become meaningless", Dr Martin writes. As we all know, when this happens, when villains get away with murder in fact, murder will be unrestrained.

Dr Martin looks at various other suggestions that have been made as to how to save the rhino, some perhaps way-out, such as manufacturing large quantities of artificial rhino horn so as to flood the market and bring down the price; others of a less speculative nature, such as establishing breeding herds of rhinos in suitable habitats, protected by electric fences and patrolled day and night by well-paid guards. The poaching situation in East Africa has become so serious that Dr Martin speculates as to whether a black rhino breeding herd should be established in another continent, on the lines of "operation oryx": the few surviving Arabian oryx were assembled at a zoo in Phoenix, Arizona, where numbers have built up so satisfactorily that some of the captive-bred animals have been taken to holding grounds in Oman, in the hope that, ultimately, they can be released in their natural environment.

Finally, Dr Martin believes that a heart-felt appeal to wholesalers who import the horn, legally or illegally, into Asian countries, to cease to do so, and perhaps substitute some other horn like that of the saiga antelope, might not fall on deaf ears. Some may consider this suggestion over-optimistic, but at least it is worth a try.

This book is, so far as I know, the first attempt to present a succinct and concise account of the trade in rhino horn and other rhino products, and it is a privilege to introduce what I believe to be an important contribution to the literature of conservation. I hope that it will not only be read and digested, but acted upon. Here is the rub. Dr Martin has found out the facts, stressed the situation's urgency and suggested measures which, although they could provide no quick or complete solution to the problem, might at least halt the decline towards extinction of this fascinating species, cursed with its myth-encrusted horn. The tendency of large organizations to generate a maximum of words and a minimum of action has not passed by the world of conservation. Good intentions, like some African rivers, are apt to run into sands of reports, committees, conferences and global strategies, which keep a lot of people busy but do not halt the poacher with his gun or poisoned arrow, the smuggler in his dhow, the importer with his faked documents.

While people pass resolutions, rhinos die.

It is to be hoped that Dr Martin's study will not only interest and intrigue his readers but will also stir into vigorous action governments, societies and individuals who really want to see the rhino preserved. "Run, rhino, run"—he is approaching the brink but it is still in our power, if only just, to halt his plunge over the precipice.

Elspeth Huxley

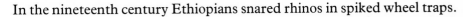

In the nineteenth century Ethiopians snared rhinos in spiked wheel traps.

1 · Rhinos in History and Mythology

Rhinoceroses have been on earth for 60 million years; fossil forms have been found in North America, Europe, Africa and Asia. Altogether, there have been at least 30 species, including the largest mammal of all time, *Baluchitherium grangeri*, which lived in Mongolia. This gigantic, hornless creature stood six metres at the shoulder, was nine metres long and probably weighed 25 tons, or four times as much as today's African bull elephant. He wandered about the Mongolian plains, browsing on leaves and branches. In the upper Miocene Age *Baluchitherium* disappeared. During the Pliocene many other forms of the rhinoceros died out, including those in North America. In the Pleistocene yet more became extinct, probably due to climatic changes and hunting by man.

Today there are only four genera and five species of the rhinoceros left. Most are threatened with extinction; all are in conflict with man.

There are three Asian species, and their total numbers are thought to be less than 2,000. The largest is the Indian, or Greater One-Horned Rhino (*Rhinoceros unicornis*), only found in northern India and southern Nepal; there are said to be about 1,500 remaining in the wild.

The Javan, or Lesser One-Horned Rhino (*Rhinoceros sondaicus*), weighs between 1,500 and 1,900 kilos (compared with 1,600 to 2,100 kilos for the Indian species). The Javan rhino is found only at the western end of Java—where there may be as few as 50 individuals left; none are in zoos. In 1850 the Lesser One-Horned Rhino still flourished throughout West Malaysia, Thailand, Viet Nam, Burma, India and most of the area of Java and Sumatra. Demand for its horn, skin and other products resulted in its wholesale extermination.

The third Asian species, the Sumatran Two-Horned Rhino (*Dicerorhinus sumatrensis*), is the smallest of all extant rhinos, weighing around 850 kilos and standing 1.3 metres at the shoulder. It is distinguished by its smooth skin, covered until maturity by a long, hairy coat. Over the past century, like the Javan rhino, its numbers have been much diminished by hunting and also by the growth of human populations which have intruded on its traditional grazing grounds. One hundred years ago the Sumatran animal was at home in much of South-East Asia, including India, Burma, Thailand, Viet Nam, Cambodia, Laos, peninsular Malaysia, Sumatra and Borneo. Today there are probably under 300 in the wild (none in zoos), with most of those remaining in Sumatra and West Malaysia. There may possibly be small populations still existing in Burma, Thailand and Borneo. When I was in Thailand in 1979, I was told by Pong Leng-Ee, Chief of the Wildlife Conservation Division of the Royal Forest Department, that rangers had seen the tracks of six Sumatran rhinos within the last few years, but that no ranger had actually seen the animal itself. I did not hear of a single person in Thailand who had come across a rhino in the wild during the past four years. Markus Borner in 1977 wrote that Sumatran rhinos still existed in Borneo, but two years later the Schenkel husband and wife team of zoologists doubted whether there were any remaining. Ken Proud, a National Parks official in Malaysia, claims that there is no evidence now of rhinos in Sarawak, which until World War II was a stronghold for the Sumatran species.

The other two rhino species live in Africa. The largest by far, in fact the largest of all living forms, is the White, or Square-Lipped Rhino (*Ceratotherium simum*). It can weigh up to 3,600 kilos and is the second largest land mammal, after the

Head lowered, a black rhino rushes forward to charge a Land Rover, a locomotive or maybe just a butterfly.

elephant. It exists in two widely separated areas: one in southern Africa, with the majority in Zululand; and the other in the Guinea savannah and deciduous woodlands of south-eastern Central African Republic, the southern Sudan, northern Zaire and, until the late 1970s, north-western Uganda as far east as the Nile. The Black Rhino (*Diceros bicornis*) weighs between 1,000 and 1,350 kilos and, unlike the grass-eating white rhino, is a browser. It probably numbered hundreds of thousands in the nineteenth century; in 1981 that figure is down to somewhere between 12,000 and 18,000.

Rhinos are represented in the earliest cave drawings in Europe, dating back some 20,000 years. However, after the last Ice Age, European man had no more rhinos to hunt, and he appears to have made no further reference to rhinos until the fifth century BC. It was then when a Greek named Ctesias wrote about a creature which had a purple head and carried a horn on its forehead. This horn was used to make drinking cups to detect poison. Ctesias was the private physician to King Artaxerxes I of Persia, but it does seem that he was rather gullible and inclined to accept statements made by informants who resorted to their imaginations when facts were lacking. For instance, he mentions a people with such gigantic feet that they lay on their backs and raised them in the air to give themselves protection from the bright sun! Ctesias' horned animal sounds like an

Archaeologists have discovered remains of early rhino species in Kansas and London, but to date the most famous cave drawings of rhinos are in Dordogne; Henri Breuil (left) shows one to colleagues.

inspired combination of an Indian ass and an Indian rhino. The reference is important though, because it shows that, over a great span of time, rhino horn has been held to have special properties.

Most of the early European myths about rhinos probably originated from Chinese tales that circulated in entrepots where rhino horn and elephant ivory were traded. Some of these were blatantly absurd, although taken for granted at the time and even elaborated upon. As an example, it was said that rhinos had no joints in their legs, and in order to sleep they propped themselves against trees in a standing position. If a rhino fell down, it could not get up, so to capture the creature all one had to do was to induce it to lean against a half-sawn-through timber which would collapse, bringing the rhino down with it. Another belief was that rhinos were fond of music and perfume. A man dressed up as a highly perfumed virgin girl was thought to be an irresistible lure to any rhino. If the disguise did not work, and instead the rhino charged, forcing the lure to climb a tree for safety, he could dissuade the beast from further attack by urinating in its ear!

Two centuries after Ctesias, Europeans were able to see live rhinos in Alexandria; these animals were probably white rhinos which may have been captured around Lake Chad. In the first century BC a Roman called Julius Maternus became the first European to cross the Sahara to the Lake Chad region. There he saw rhinos in the wild. "We can imagine the Roman watching with amazement," commented one writer, "as the huge creatures, squealing and puffing, chased each other around in the strong light of the desert moon." In 11 BC an Indian ruler presented Emperor Augustus with a Greater One-Horned Rhino, and soon afterwards Romans began sending out their own expeditions to West Africa to bring back rhinos for public exhibition. The poet Marcus Valerius Martialis commented that they were the most aggressive fighters of all the animals in the Roman arenas; sometimes, he said, they even impaled bears with their horns and tossed them over their backs.

After the collapse of the Roman Empire and later with the rise of Islam, Europe was cut off from the Middle East and the Orient and no longer had access to tropical animals. Fantasy and wild imagination ran rampant in descriptions of African and Asiatic beasts. Where rhinos were concerned, poets, historians and geographers in the Dark Ages made a distorted identification with the mythical unicorn, a legendary animal whose horn was said to be a general panacea for all types of diseases and ailments.

The unicorn entered European mythology at an early date; both Aristotle and Pliny were convinced of its existence. The creature was usually believed to be the size of a small horse with a beard and a pointed horn of one metre or more in length protruding from its forehead. Like the rhino, the unicorn was endowed with enormous strength, but this was concentrated in its single horn. The unicorn was said to precede other animals to water and to render it pure by dipping the tip of its horn into it. Here is an obvious analogy to rhino horn which was believed capable of rendering some poisons harmless. There is also another link between conceptions of the rhino and conceptions of the unicorn: at the mythical level both seem to exist only in the male form. One Roman writer adamantly declared that all rhinos were males (engendered by rocks!). The unicorn, for its part, was 'known' to be irresistibly attracted to virgin girls. Leonardo da Vinci believed that only a young virgin could capture a unicorn, and then only momentarily. To do so, she had to sit in a forest, quietly by herself, with one breast bared. A unicorn would come to her and place his head in her lap long enough to allow her to pluck the horn from his forehead.

'Unicorn horn' could once be purchased from dealers in Europe. It had two quite different sources. The first came from the frozen waters of the north, passing through the hands of many traders who had never seen the animal from which it was taken, for not even the Greeks had ventured to the Arctic, the home of the narwhal. The males of this whale species sport a long spirally tooth, a kind of ivory tusk which does indeed look like a horn and was readily accepted as the unicorn's horn. The second source was in fact rhino horn, from Africa and Asia and vaguely associated with the memories of the exotic beasts about which the Romans had written. Although there were no similarities between the appearance of these two horns, both were thought to have the same qualities. It also seems that later on rhino horn became more prevalent on the European markets and that rhinos, for a while, were synonymous with unicorns. In 1298 the celebrated Venetian traveller, Marco Polo, accepted the rhinos on the island of Sumatra as unicorns, despite their ungainly appearance:

> There are wild elephants in the country, and numerous unicorns, which are very nearly as big. They have hair like that of a buffalo, feet like those of an elephant, and a horn in the middle of the forehead, which is black and very thick … They delight much to abide in mire and mud. 'Tis a passing ugly beast to look upon, and is not in the least like that which our stories tell of being caught in the lap of a virgin; in fact, 'tis altogether different from what we fancy.

Arab traders, realizing the value of rhino horns in Europe, acted as middlemen to procure many Indian rhino horns from Asia. The Arabs claimed them as unicorn horns when they sold them to respected and influential European importers. Retail pharmacists then made fortunes by attesting to the medicinal powers of the supposed unicorn horn. The pharmacists ground the horn into a powder that went into a pomade used to treat a variety of ailments. Craftsmen also purchased the horn from the importers for making drinking cups, salt-cellars and spoons.

The 'unicorn horn' was an important drug for hundreds of years in Europe; both the rich and the poor consumed it. Many churches and wealthy men possessed an entire horn: Queen Elizabeth I had one in her bedroom at Windsor, which was one of her most valuable possessions. In 1741 unicorn horn was still an officially recognized drug in England, and as late as 1789 the French court was still using 'unicorn horns' to test the royal food to see if poison had been added. All these were rhino horns, and even a Pope had one: in 1591 Pope Gregory XIV, on his deathbed, was offered a horn from an Indian rhino. The tip of the horn was ground down into a powder and fed to him, but the desired effect did not take place. Shortly after consuming the potion, he died. This particular horn has been preserved for posterity and is presently in the Museum of Natural History in New York.

The alleged power of the unicorn horn led to its adoption as the symbol of the apothecary trade in Western Europe. Even today, Burroughs Wellcome, one of the world's largest pharmaceutical companies, uses a unicorn as its trademark. A friend of mine was recently given an electric toaster by Wellcome Trust Research Laboratories in Nairobi—with a unicorn emblazoned on it.

The first live rhino in Europe after the Fall of the Roman Empire appeared in 1515 when King Muzaffar of Cambay in western India sent one as a gift to King Manuel of Portugal. After a few months the Portuguese monarch decided to send the creature on to Pope Leo X; and, in order to make the present even more spectacular, he harnessed the rhino in a green velvet collar, studded with gold roses and carnations, attached to a gilt iron chain. When the ship carrying the wondrous animal put into Marseilles, Francis I happened to be there and instructed the captain, with the help of a bribe of 5,000 gold crowns, to take the rhino off and display it to the populace. Later, when the rhino was safely aboard again, the ship left for Rome, but a storm blew up and the ship was wrecked off

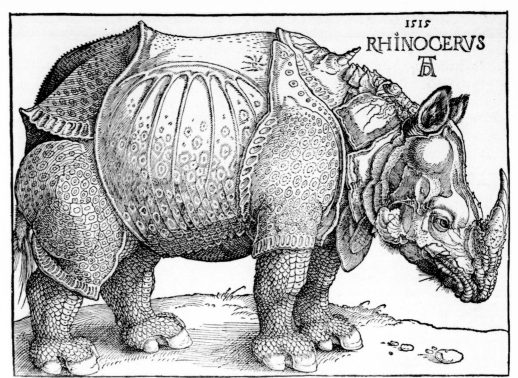

Albrecht Dürer never saw the Indian rhino on which he based his famous woodcut in 1515; at this time rhinos were confused with the mythical unicorn, hence the small spiral horn on the rhino's shoulder.

Genoa, resulting in the loss of all lives. The carcass of the rhino drifted ashore, where it was picked up, skinned, stuffed and forwarded anyway to Rome for the Pope to see.

Whilst this Indian rhino had been in Lisbon, an artist sketched it and his drawing later found its way to Augsburg and into the hands of the painter Albrecht Dürer, who also obtained a first-hand description of the rhino in a letter sent to him. In turn, Dürer produced his famous woodcut in 1515 of a rhinoceros; even though it was not very accurate, it remained the standard representation of the Indian rhino for more than 200 years and was copied many times by lesser masters.

In the eighteenth century another Indian rhino appeared with fanfare on the European scene, causing a tremendous sensation. An enterprising Dutchman named Douvemont van der Meer imported it and toured it around the capital cities in the 1740s. Besides feeding the rhino a regular diet of hay, van der Meer also gave his pet large quantities of beer and wine. The high point of the tour was when the rhino was led into Vienna with a full honour guard. Christian Gellert wrote a poem about this animal, Oudry painted it, Charpentier engraved it and Casanova included it in an episode of his memoirs. Louis XV tried to purchase the rhino after it was exhibited at Versailles in a specially built cage on wheels drawn by eight horses. However, van der Meer wanted 100,000 écus for his prodigious beast, and such a sum was too exorbitant even for the King's menagerie. So, Madame de Pompadour contented herself with tossing orange peels into its mouth during the short visit, and praised its facial features.

Although the Indian rhino became known once again to the European aristocracy during the Renaissance and several had been exhibited by the end of the eighteenth century, neither of the African species became familiar specimens until much later. One did come in 1868, however, a black rhino purchased by the 40-year-old Regent's Park Zoo. It was studied by the great zoologist Sclater and drawn by Joseph Wolf. It is a curious historical note that when the West's first modern zoological gardens were opened in the nineteenth century, the African rhino was much more of a rarity than the Indian one. Today a pair of Indian rhinos can change hands for $150,000—more than three times the amount that zoos now pay for black rhinos.

The Indian rhinos of old have a much more colourful history than their African counterparts. Aside from the pharmaceutical uses to which rhinos have been put for thousands of years in Asia, there are wondrous chronicles about rhinos as beasts of warfare. Indian rhinos with iron tridents attached to their horns were put in the front lines of the Indian armies to disperse enemy troops. When the notorious Tamerlane conquered Delhi in 1398, he was met by King Mohamed Nassir ed Din's twelve tame rhinos, which all lowered their heads in respect to the great Mongol warrior. This magnificent gesture had no effect on Tamerlane, for soon afterwards he massacred 100,000 prisoners in the city.

Tame Indian rhinos were also used in circuses and kept as pets by the influential and the wealthy. In Assam domesticated rhinos were trained to pull ploughs. There was once even a rhino that carried laundry around the town of Gauhati in the late nineteenth century.

The only reference I have found pertaining to any kind of a rhino cult comes from Dillon Ripley, Secretary of the Smithsonian Institution:

> There is even said to be an obscure Indian religious rite, a sort of purge, performed by squatting inside the body cavity of a freshly killed rhino after it has been eviscerated. Certain prayers are recited and the severed rhino horn is used as a cup to hold the rhino blood offered to the gods.

Some Africans also believed that rhino blood had magical properties. Captain C.R.S. Pitman, describing a trip in the 1920s along the Kerio river in East Africa, wrote:

> A particularly unsavoury custom to which I was introduced by some of my voluntary assistants in the course of this trip was that of bathing in rhinoceros blood! It is even more disgusting than it sounds... Two natives indulged in this luxury, so I was told, to acquire unlimited courage and strength. As soon as the rhinoceros had breathed its last the throat was cut and the jugular severed, the skin below the gash being pulled outwards to leave a capacious hollow, which was speedily filled with blood—foul-smelling, evil-looking, and black, more viscid than fluid. Having stripped themselves of their scanty body adornments, these two savages, with evident delight, smeared themselves from head to toe with the filthy slime till they reeked with offensiveness and literally shone in the brilliant sunshine.

People living in longhouses in inland Borneo revere dried rhino penises alongside sacred stones and bones in religious fertility ceremonies. The Sumatran rhino penis has a crossbar, known locally as a *palang*, ten centimetres below the tip; the crossbar extends five centimetres on either side. Traditionally, and until quite recently, Kenyah and Kelabit tribesmen in Borneo pierced their own penises in order to insert a piece of bamboo, bone or wood as a crossbar. At the ends of the crossbar they attached knobs of various types. Could it possibly be that this bizarre practice originated from the men copying what they saw in the male Sumatran rhino? Certainly, their belief in the supernatural power of rhinos was responsible for some other curious practices. For example, they used to hang a rhino's tail in a room where a woman was in labour, thinking that it would ease the pains of childbirth. In severe cases they held a rhino's penis over the woman's head and poured water through it. The alleged magic of the Sumatran rhino has obviously not helped its own survival.

When it is available, water attracts black rhinos, perhaps more for wallowing than drinking. Black rhinos can go for extended periods without free water, obtaining their requirements from plants.

One of the most famous animal trappers of all time, Carl Hagenbeck, sold this black rhino to the London zoo in 1868 for $5,000. Joseph Wolf painted it in 1872. Sclater, the secretary to the Royal Zoological Society, believed this rhino to be the first of its species to arrive alive in Europe since the days of the Roman Empire.

This Indian rhino, bought in Calcutta for the London zoo in 1864, was painted by Joseph Wolf in 1872. Its Latin name, *unicornis*, ascribed by the founder of modern taxonomy, Linnaeus, reveals the age-old mythical connection between the rhino and the unicorn.

J Wolf del. J Smit lith.

M & N Hanhart imp

RHINOCEROS UNICORNIS

RHINOCEROS SONDAICUS

The subject of this drawing by Joseph Wolf was a Javan rhino that had been kept in a tea garden in Djakarta before being purchased by the London zoo in 1874. The Javan rhino is closely related to the Indian species, and did in fact exist in Bengal until the twentieth century. It is also very fond of water and has been seen wading into the ocean to feed on mangroves.

In 1872 the London zoo purchased a Sumatran rhino for $3,000, which Joseph Wolf immediately painted, using poetic licence in that he showed two of the species in his water-colour. It was somewhat ironical: the animal, an elderly female with no lower incisors, died six weeks after arrival.

2 · The Anti-Social Rhino

Black rhinos seek sandy or dusty depressions for lying down to rest during the heat of the day. They often lie on their brisket with their legs curled under them.

Of the five rhino species, zoologists have only studied the Indian, black and white in the wild. The Javan and Sumatran rhinos have proved too difficult to get close enough to observe their behaviour. A Swiss scientist, Markus Borner, recently completed three years of research in Gunung Leuser trying to study the Sumatran rhinos. During his entire stay, he saw only one rhino for fifteen seconds, totally unexpectedly when the creature passed by his campsite.

In this chapter I will discuss just two of the rhino species, the Indian and the black, on which some of the most interesting research has been carried out. I have chosen these two to illustrate rhino behaviour also because they are the ones I have personally observed in India and East Africa.

The most detailed work on the Greater One-Horned Rhinoceros was carried out by Andrew Laurie from 1972 to 1976 in the Chitawan valley of southern Nepal. Dr Laurie's resultant dissertation for Cambridge University is of excellent scholarship, and much of what follows here on the Indian rhino comes from this unpublished source.

The massive Indian rhinoceros has a thick skin which has several folds on the neck, forequarters and in front of the hindquarters, giving the impression that the animal is covered in some sort of armour. The bellicose appearance is further enhanced by the presence of tubercles looking like iron rivets. In fact, until the twentieth century many people believed that the Greater One-Horned Rhino was bullet-proof. During the Indian Mutiny a soldier was faced with a court martial for killing a tame rhinoceros captured by his regiment; the soldier's defence was that he shot the rhino to see if it really was impervious to gunshot since he had been told that it was.

Some twentieth-century zoologists and conservationists have surmised that the warlike appearance of the Indian rhino is highly deceptive and that the animal is timid, shy and inoffensive; but Andrew Laurie's study has shown that this species is not at all placid. Because the Indian rhino prefers solitude (90 per cent of those Laurie observed were alone, aside from cow-calf pairs), many encounters between individuals are very aggressive. Whilst fights are not ordinarily lethal, they can result in serious injury. The Indian rhinos display and posture, stare and wheel, curl their lips and display their tushes (long and pointed incisor teeth). These displays usually lead to one giving way and fleeing. The victor, particularly if a male, may pursue the vanquished. If neither gives way, a real fight develops. There can be a clash between the two animals' horns or a horn and a flank. More often than not, however, no horn contact is made at all: the most dangerous part of the conflict is instead the forward and sideway rushes made with tushes bared and aimed at the opponent's head, although sometimes striking his rump or sides. The confrontations are accompanied by honks, bleats and roars, for the species is very vocal.

The rhino on the left in this nineteenth-century etching depicts the way Indian rhinos bare their tushes in display.

Courtship is also marked by violence. A female becomes sexually mature when she is seven years old. In most instances when a male approaches a female, even if she is in oestrus, she will try to drive him away, and will often succeed in repelling him. However, when she does not, horn-to-horn encounters result, from which the female will finally flee, with the male giving chase over long distances, squeaking and panting all the way. When they meet again they often turn and face each other and attempt to push each other backward, roaring between lunges and tush displays. After a while, they both take a break. Generally it is the male who

During copulation the female white rhino walks about and the male has to keep up with her. In this case, she has walked under a tree that the male cannot negotiate and he is about to fall off.

gets things going again so that, eventually, exhausted from all the activity, the female just lies down submissively. This being achieved, the male either lies down next to her himself, or stands over her, biting the air. Once Dr Laurie saw a male place his head under a female's neck and push her over onto her back; she remained still and the male stood looking at her for a minute and then turned and walked away.

Finally, the aggressive nature of both animals in courtship gives way to a more peaceful acceptance. Prior to mating the male rests his chin on the female's rump and tries to keep it there even if she begins to walk away. Both urinate frequently, and sometimes the female becomes quite excited, squeaking and panting and even forcing her head between the male's hind legs to sniff his penis.

The mounting by the male is extremely awkward and takes a long time to complete successfully. In trying to get into position he has to launch himself forward on his hind feet and get his front feet on her back. When he does not manage to raise himself sufficiently, he ends up bumping his neck on her rump, but the main problem appears to be the male's difficulty in keeping on top of the female once he is there. Often she moves forward, and he shuffles along behind her on two feet, trying to stay in step with her. His efforts may unbalance him, causing an ignominious belly flop.

Copulation, once started, may last for an hour or more. The male's ears flap and he grunts between spasms which occur every minute or so; the female, in Laurie's words, "gasps like a fish". It is fairly well known that the act of copulation lasts a relatively long time (elephants copulate for only a matter of seconds), which has given rise to the belief that the rhino possesses a tremendous sexual strength. The

22

idea that has developed from this is that because of the sexual activity of the rhino, its somewhat phallic-shaped horn can be used as a sexual stimulant for humans when it is ground down into a powder. What this does not take account of is how monumentally clumsy and inept the male is in making love to his mate; if the facts were better known perhaps some of the myths would disappear.

The rhino calf is born after a gestation period of about sixteen months. The mother stays with her calf for three to four years and steers clear of other rhinos during this time, except for brief encounters at wallowing pools. Soon after birth the calf is able to stand and it moves towards its mother for milk. Calves are quite active and interested in their surroundings, sniffing at different plants and occasionally picking up sticks in their mouths. Sometimes they approach other rhinos, whom the mothers are quick to chase away. At one year the infant calves have been weaned, a stage at which they are in real danger of being attacked by adult males. Male juveniles are particularly prone to attack, perhaps because they are looked upon by the adults as potential rivals. The result is that male juveniles tend to stay with their mothers longer than females.

Passing from adolescence to adulthood, the male rhino increasingly likes to be on his own, only occasionally meeting up with his fellows at wallows and feeding grounds. Indian rhinos are not really territorial animals. Dr Laurie believes that because of the animal's poor eyesight and the tendency of males to roam vast ranges in search of females and food, efforts to defend a specific area are impractical.

Adult Indian rhinos are both grazers and browsers. Grass makes up about four-fifths of their diet; the rest consists of fruits, leaves, branches, shrubs, aquatic plants and agricultural crops. On average, Indian rhinos spend about 45 per cent of their time feeding, almost 30 per cent resting, and the remaining 25 per cent in such activities as wallowing, getting to know other rhinos, standing alert to danger and moving around. Night-time is popular for feeding. Resting usually occupies the morning hours from 8 am until noon.

Indian rhinos love water, but they have rather messy habits in it. Unlike elephants who always face upstream, rhinos pay no attention to which way the water is flowing, and urinate and defecate at the same time as they drink. The percentage of time spent in water of course varies between the cold winter season when wallowing goes somewhat out of fashion and the hot monsoon months from June to September when rain is frequent and lakes build up.

Watching rhinos wallow is a hilarious sight; they abandon themselves wholly to the fun, rolling over and thrashing about with their legs in the air. When they want to move from one side to the other, they stand up first, gaze about and then lie down again. Depending on the weather and his mood, a rhino can spend as little as a few minutes or as long as seven hours in the water at any one time. A favourite pastime of every rhino is to rub his rump in the mud, sitting in dog-like fashion as he does so.

Wallowing serves several purposes: the water lowers the rhino's body temperature; prevents fly-bites to some extent; and, since wallowing places are popular, sociable, even friendly meetings can occur. Fights are not so common at water-holes as they are when rhinos suddenly meet up with one another in the bush.

The possible lifespan of an Indian rhino in the wild is not known. Of the six dead rhinos that Dr Laurie examined in Chitawan, the oldest was estimated to be 26 years. However, there are records of Indian rhinos living in captivity for much longer periods. For instance, I saw in the Trivandrum zoo in southern India a male rhino that the authorities claimed they had had for 49 years.

The major causes of death to Indian rhinos in Nepal in the 1970s were poaching, fighting among themselves, abandonment of calves by their mothers and killing of

Although this rhino seemingly enjoys solitary comfort at his wallow, as many as nine Indian rhinos may sometimes be seen together at the same wallow.

calves by tigers. Between 1970 and 1972 poachers took seventeen rhinos in Chitawan Park, but the rhinos themselves sometimes take revenge on people. In the mid 1970s five villagers lost their lives to rhinos on the borders of Chitawan. At night rhinos come out of the park and graze on the adjoining fields of wheat, maize and rice. Farmers have been forced to employ nightwatchmen to patrol their land; they stand on platforms overlooking the fields and sound the alarm whenever a rhino appears. To frighten away the rhinos they wave flame torches, make a lot of noise and sometimes they resort to trying to push a rhino out of a field. Often a rhino will leave only to wander onto another nearby farm where the guard happens to be asleep. The damage caused by raiding rhinos is considerable: as much as 20 per cent of the rice crop grown near the park boundaries is lost to them every year.

Despite the problems of poaching and other risks, the number of Indian rhinos in Nepal and India has recently been on the increase: possibly six per cent a year in Chitawan alone. Barring unforeseen political changes, the Indian rhinoceros should continue to prosper in reserves and parks.

Unfortunately, the outlook for the black rhino in Africa is not so encouraging. Although it is the most common and most numerous rhino species in the world, it has been hardest hit by indiscriminate killing. Around 90 per cent of all black rhinos in East Africa (the region with the largest populations) died between 1970 and 1980. Moreover, today, breeding in the wild is very much on the decline. Research is desperately needed to try to discover why, and to work out what should be done to render conditions more favourable for natural increase.

Having lived in East Africa for the past eighteen years, I am far more familiar with the black rhino than other species. With my wife, Chryssee, an Honorary Warden for Kenya National Parks from 1971 to 1976, I have made many trips to national parks and reserves in the region, and in those days we used to come across rhinos regularly.

Undoubtedly, the most endearing rhino we ever knew was Rufus, an orphaned male who was brought up by the Kearneys, and later by Daphne Sheldrick, in Tsavo East National Park. Rufus first appeared inside the Kearneys' cook's hut, a tiny calf who had obviously lost his mother and was looking for company. He was given a milk formula, to which he readily took, and soon also began munching lucerne. When Daphne Sheldrick took him over from the Kearneys, who were transferred to Nairobi Park, she decided that in Rufus' own interest he should be introduced to natural vegetation so that he could eventually be returned to the wild, although she did not prohibit the special titbits that he favoured.

One of Rufus' greatest pleasures in life was his daily bath; he very much enjoyed wallowing in mud and having his back scrubbed by humans. Another treat for Rufus was eating sweets. When Chryssee and I drove down to the coast we would always go shopping for Rufus beforehand. On arrival at Voi, we would find out where Rufus was from a ranger on duty at the park gate, and then we would drive on to see him. He would be with a herd of other orphaned wild animals, and as soon as we caught a glimpse of him, Chryssee would jump out of the Land Rover and call to him. Leaving his companions, he would trot right up to her and let her hand feed him candy and fruit. He was very gentle and would show affection by leaning slightly and rubbing his head or flank against his friend, the bearer of gifts. After consuming a pound-box of imported English chocolates and several oranges, off he would wander back to the other orphans. In the late afternoon, when the sun was going down, it was an extraordinary sight to watch a couple of rangers herding in single file a group of partly tame animals back to stables at the park's headquarters: Rufus the rhino, a zebra, two ostriches, several buffaloes and an elephant.

Rufus' demise is a sad story. Daphne Sheldrick has written that Rufus was "the most docile and placid animal I have ever known, and children could ride him and handle him with safety"; but one day he turned on one of his keepers. A substitute man, hired to look after the animals during the day when they grazed in the park,

Orphaned black rhinos readily make friends with other animals. This one has not charged his zebra playmate, but has taken advantage of its recumbent position to rub his chin on it.

disliked Rufus for some reason and often beat him with a stick. One afternoon when this man was sharing duty with an old Turkana who knew and treated the wild animals very well, Rufus attacked. The man screamed for assistance and the old Turkana came over to help. We can only surmise that Rufus had become so enraged with the constant beatings that he failed to notice that the old man had come between him and his adversary; in his attempt to get at his enemy he instead caught his horn in the thigh of the old Turkana. The old man was rushed to hospital at Voi but bled to death that night. Rufus was consequently banished to a forlorn corner of the park to try to survive on his own.

The inevitable occurred.

A few days later he probably just walked up to play with some wild animals, having become accustomed to several unlikely companions. Unfortunately, he chose a pride of lions which, in their astonishment, attacked him fiercely, savagely lacerating his body. Rufus died a slow and agonizing death.

This is not an unusual tale: wild animals brought up by humans are often unable to defend themselves from predators. Rufus should probably not have been released into an area of the park that he did not know without some sort of protection or supervision.

Despite its ungainly appearance, the black rhino is a power-house of muscles. As part of his anatomical study of rhinos, Jonathan Kingdon has produced many drawings of the remarkable muscle structure of this animal which enables it to execute abrupt turns even when charging at speeds up to 50 kilometres an hour.

Tales are legendary about black rhinos charging at anything—even butterflies. Kingdon suggests (and the number of wrecked Land Rovers supports this view point) that rhinos will go out of their way to seek contact with large moving vehicles. They also often head for camp fires and curiously scatter burning logs with their horns.

The work of the best known popularizer of elephant behaviour, Iain Douglas-Hamilton, was almost cut short by a charging rhino in Lake Manyara Park in 1967. He was following on foot the spoor of a group of elephants when suddenly a female rhino came crashing through the undergrowth towards him, accompanied by her very large calf. Iain turned and ran as fast as he could through the bushes, swerving sharply in an attempt to get the rhinos off his trail, but to no avail; his sandal broke and he fell to the ground, face downwards. The mother rhino rushed at him and kicked him hard in the back, producing a massive haemorrhage. At that point Iain lost consciousness and can only guess that the rhinos soon lost interest in his inert body and moved away.

The black rhino does have some peculiar habits. He tends to defecate in only certain spots in his home range. Since any other rhino passing by will make use of the same place, it is not truly a territorial marking. Tremendous mounds build up. When a rhino finishes defecating, he spreads the droppings around by treading through them with his hind feet. Some Africans told A.T. Ritchie, Chief Game Warden of Kenya from 1923 to 1948, that the reason rhinos disperse their dung is that elephants do not like to see droppings lying about similar to their own. A more scientific explanation, given by John Goddard, is that because the rhino has poor eyesight he might well use the droppings as a scent trail. It is apparent that the middens have special significance to rhinos; perhaps their purpose is to give individuals the choice of seeking or avoiding contact with one another.

Urinating, where males are concerned, also seems to have special meaning. In the presence of his fellows, a male 'shows off' by thrusting his penis backwards between his hind legs and letting loose a burst of urine with such force as to send it spraying for three or four metres. When he is alone, the male urinates in a more downward fashion and often onto bushes or shrubs that he backs up to; sometimes he even attacks the bush and tramples it afterwards. Ritchie reported that in

This white rhino cow shares a dung heap with a sub-adult male; scientists are still uncertain why some rhinos tend to defecate in the same place.

certain dry areas of Kenya and Somalia rhinos have favourite stones on which they urinate, rather like a dog that has a favourite tree.

Much has been said by the few scientists who have observed rhinos eating wildebeest dung. They think that the rhino does this because there may be some sort of mineral in it that appeals to him; but Jonathan Kingdon's anatomy study probably provides a better answer. The black rhino has a prehensile upper lip that helps him to gather twigs into his mouth, but it is disadvantageous for cropping short grass; consuming wildebeest dung could provide him with the bulk that he needs in the dry season when tall grass is just not available.

In studying rhinos in Ngorongoro Crater, Olduvai Gorge and Tsavo, Goddard established that the population in each place was falling. The seven to ten per cent additional young each year did not compensate for the high death rate. And, of course, at the time when Goddard was carrying out his research, poaching was not as serious a threat as it was later to become.

Many rhino deaths are caused by other wild animals. Hyenas are the major predators of young rhino calves, and lions take their toll, too. Actually, the black rhino calf is much more vulnerable than the square-lipped one which walks in front of his mother, thus staying within her view. The black, instead, always follows his mother, and a predator can more easily carry out its attack before the mother realizes what is happening. Often, she is alerted to the danger only after her calf has fallen prey and begins to squeal.

Hippos and buffaloes have occasionally been known to kill adult rhinos, and, in periods of drought, rhinos almost always lose out to elephants. In fact, elephants are generally a menace to rhinos. Sometimes they appear to harass rhinos just for the fun of doing so, as Philip Keller described in *Africa's Wild Glory*. Four young bull elephants that Keller had been watching found an old rhino enjoying a dust bath. They had seen him drive away a cow with a calf from the coveted spot and waited until he had settled in comfortably. The elephants then slowly moved up towards him, almost forming a circle around the area. As if the rhino predicted what would happen, he began snorting violently in protest. In unison the elephants began kicking up the dust with their gigantic feet, drawing in more with their trunks and squirting it all over the unfortunate prostrate creature. Finally, with a roar he got up and ran away from the suffocating cloud. Shortly afterwards, the elephants moved off, and Keller wrote that "the way the elephants dangled their tails back and forth as they minced away convinced me that they had enjoyed the prank immensely and were only laughing up their trunks at the truculent old 'sobersides'".

At other times elephants show a more vehement dislike for rhinos. In 1979 at the Ark Lodge, which faces a water-hole favoured by many species in the Aberdare National Park and which has become a kind of 'second Treetops', a dramatic fight took place. The incident started one evening around midnight, when sixteen elephants came to the water-hole for a drink. They noticed an adult male rhino already drinking there and gave chase to him. Soon afterwards a female rhino with a calf arrived. The calf began to play with one of the young elephants which annoyed an already petulant mother elephant who picked up the rhino calf with her trunk and literally threw the creature into the forest. Still not satisfied, the elephant attempted to impale it with her tusks, but at that moment the rhino mother charged the elephant, distracting her and permitting the calf to escape. As soon as she realized that it was safe she turned and ran off as well. Meanwhile, all the commotion had attracted the male rhino back to the water-hole. The mother elephant was not about to tolerate any interference from him again, so she charged him at great speed and succeeded in tossing him three metres into the air and finishing him off when he landed by kneeling on him and thrusting one of her tusks through his chest. Her rage continued until she had pushed the rhino's body into the water-hole, whereupon she calmly walked away. The next morning twenty men and a tractor were required to move the rhino carcass from the water.

Such hunting scenes were recorded by many of the early European explorers to Africa and may have accounted for the onset of the rhinos' demise.

28

3 · The Slaughter of Rhinos

1 The Asian Species

Westerners have been amused, awed, amazed and often embarrassed by the friendship shown by the people of Asia to their animals. Perhaps this friendship was born of necessity; certainly, the elephant and the camel have traditionally played a much more important role in Eastern civilizations than the horse has in the West. Moreover, Hindus, Buddhists, and Muslims often treat their animals with a kindness which is much greater than their respect for them. Westerners do not truly understand this; and the concept that gods, dragons, animals and men may be united in a marvellous world where fantasy and reality are entwined is very Eastern. Westerners may have derived literary inspiration from ideas like this, but they are alien to Western culture.

Whatever mystic link may have existed between animal and man in the West was defiantly broken at the time of the Reformation, when saints with their birds and lions were pushed aside to give man his unique and dominant place in Creation. The Age of Reason went so far as to proclaim that animals were bereft of soul and consequently incapable of feeling pain, desire or pleasure.

Of course, in the East, despite beliefs that man should do no harm to beast or bug, there has always been some hunting; unfortunately, the Indian rhino was never endowed with characteristics which gave it immunity from the hunt. It served no domestic purpose nor held any particular religious significance, although among Hindus and Buddhists the elephant reached the celestial realm. Even among the less anthropomorphic Muslims, animals accomplished miraculous feats. But the rhino was denied all this; for example, unlike the camel, it had no hope of learning Mohamed's hundredth name for Allah.

When the first great marauders of Indian wildlife came along, the foreign Mongols, rhinos immediately became targets. Tamerlane massacred rhinos on the present Kashmir border. Babur, the conqueror of northern India, took great delight in describing his rhino hunts in 1525, close to the Khyber Pass. He also tried to get a tame elephant to fight a rhino and was sorely disappointed when the latter ran off into the bush without even so much as an attempt to charge the elephant. Babur's son, Humayun, liked chasing rhinos from horseback, shooting arrows into them.

At the time of Emperor Babur, the Indian rhino was still widespread, from the Indus river in the west to Burma in the east. But already in the sixteenth century human populations were increasing and the rhino had to give way to new settlements in fertile flood plains and lowland grass areas, which he so favoured. Then, from the middle of the nineteenth century to the year 1900, there was such a slaughter of Indian rhinos by sportsmen that their numbers were reduced to only a few hundred. As early as 1850 no rhinos were left in the Rajmahal hills of Bihar, and, in 1878, the last rhino was shot in Uttar Pradesh. By 1890 Indian rhinos had vanished from most areas except southern Nepal, the Bhutan Duars, parts of West Bengal and the Brahmaputra valley of Assam. As late as 1896, the government of Bengal was paying a bounty of 20 rupees for every rhino killed.

It was the introduction of modern fire-arms by British military officers which was the rhino's undoing. Great sport (and prestige amongst one's peers) was to be had from the back of an elephant trained to stand its ground when face to face with a rhino. One method was quietly to track a rhino to his lair, shooting him dead when he was standing quite unconscious of any danger. Another technique involved "beating him out of the jungle with a line of elephants, the guns being stationed at the points where he is most likely to break cover", which General Kinloch seemed to prefer. One drawback of this strategy was that it was necessary "to have reliable men with the beaters, who can exercise authority and keep them in order, for both mahouts and elephants have the greatest dread of the huge brute, who appears to be much more formidable that he really is". Many of the British military officers belittled the rhino, calling him a stupid beast, and it seems surprising that they enjoyed hunting him so much. Colonel Fitzwilliam Thomas Pollok, who wrote three books on hunting in India, admitted, "I waged war against those pachyderms, why, I don't know". According to his own count, he killed at least 47 rhinos in Assam and Bengal. He also left uncounted numbers of wounded ones, as the following excerpt from his *Incidents of Foreign Sport and Travel* illustrates:

> . . . when passing a strip of long elephant grass J. [Jackson, Pollok's fellow officer in the Indian Army and hunting companion] caught sight of a rhino and fired. It began to spin round and round, and to emit the sounds elephants dread so much, and to our amazement, from a patch of long grass close at hand, fully a dozen more rhino joined the chorus! I never heard such a pandemonium in my life! If the inmates of a lunatic asylum and a dozen menageries had been let loose and intermingled the row could not have been more deafening. Not an elephant with us would stir a step forward, the grass was dense and high, and so full of brutes in a state of frenzy that I did not like to force our mounts forward. After the row ceased, they were willing to enter the cover, but I was afraid of getting them cut. We tried to set the grass on fire, but the dew was still on it, and it would not burn.

Not to be outdone by the British, the Maharajah of Cooch Behar shot 207 rhinos between 1871 and 1907 in West Bengal and Assam. In his book, *Thirty-seven Years of Big Game Shooting*, this Maharajah proudly recalls "a magnificent day's sport" near Rossik Bheel and Cheugtimari, "when we bagged five rhinos before luncheon. I do not think that this record has been beaten."

Aside from hunting for sport, which undoubtedly was the main cause of the demise of Indian rhino populations in the nineteenth century, the luckless creature was also threatened by another and more subtle foe: tea. The British had acquired their taste for tea in the middle of the eighteenth century. By 1783 they were importing three million kilos of it, and just two years later the amount jumped to seven million kilos; it was almost 14 million kilos in 1800. The East India Company found tea its most profitable import into Britain and was comforted by the thought that it did not adversely affect the development of industry at home.

Wild tea plants had been discovered growing in Assam, but there was some doubt as to whether or not they constituted 'real' tea, so at first the East India Company imported Chinese plants to Assam. There was, however, considerable difficulty in trying to clear the land of Indian tea to make space for the Chinese. The local variety would not be easily ousted, and finally the E.I.C. decided to cultivate Indian tea for export. It proved popular and the trade flourished as never imagined. By 1900 Britain was importing 62 million kilos of black tea from India as against 11 million kilos of green tea from China.

To grow tea commercially, vast tracts of land are needed for plantations. Assam has an ideal climate for tea and the advantage of being one of the more sparsely populated areas of India. The result was that towards the middle of the nineteenth century speculators were frantically bidding for tea estates in the unmapped jungle. Later, when the first tea was ready to be picked, labour had to be found.

In a rhino fight organized by the Maharajah in Baroda, India, for entertainment, the European artist mistakenly gave the rhinos two horns each. It was not an uncommon error; differentiating rhino species was quite a problem until this century.

Great numbers of Biharis, Madrassis and Bengalis were imported to Assam, where they were kept in concentration camp conditions. In one 18-month period 18,000 out of 150,000 'coolies' died or vanished in the wilds of Assam.

Conditions did gradually improve for the labourers, but day by day worsened for the rhino. The transformation of his habitat, the tremendous influx of people and, finally, a railway linking Assam with other parts of India left little chance for his continued survival. By 1908 there were only twelve rhinos left alive in the Kaziranga area of central Assam, which had once had the greatest concentration of these animals.

In Nepal, the Indian rhino populations did not approach extinction until the middle of the twentieth century. Then, during winter seasons, members of the Rana family, the hereditary prime ministers of Nepal, began to make a practice of going into the Chitawan valley to hunt rhinos and tigers. As hunting became a more popular sport, these Maharajahs occasionally invited British V.I.P.s to accompany them. The scale of the operation grew and sometimes hundreds of domestic elephants were used in these hunts. In the 1937/8 season alone, 38 rhinos and 120 tigers were shot.

In 1939, the late Armand Denis, world-renowned wildlife film-maker, visited the Maharajah in Kathmandu. The Maharajah eagerly showed him his trophy room inside the palace. This consisted of a hall some 40 feet long. On one of the walls was a gigantic mural, painted by a Frenchman, depicting the Maharajah hunting rhinos. On each side of the hall were 20 marble pillars, on top each of which rested the stuffed head of a rhino—40 rhinos in all! Repulsed by this sight, Armand Denis turned to the Maharajah and said: "You are aware, of course, Your Highness, that there are very, very few of these animals left". The Maharajah took a little time to answer, then turned to his guest, winked and replied: "I think you will find that there will be just enough to last me my lifetime".

In 1951 the Rana regime, after deposing the King, fell, leaving in its wake administrative chaos. Poaching began on a grand scale; lesser men took revenge on their former masters by slaughtering 'royal game'. At least 75 rhinos were killed by poachers in 1959 and similar numbers were taken in the previous few years. In 1960, E.P. Gee estimated that another 75 Indian rhinos were illegally killed in Chitawan; by 1961 he believed that there were no more than 160 left alive there. Moreover, because of the lack of control in the country, farmers from the hills descended into the fertile Chitawan valley to settle. Between 1950 and 1960 the human population of the valley rose from 36,000 to 100,000, and 70 per cent of the forests and grasslands were cleared for cultivation, destroying much of the rhino's natural environment.

Finally, in the mid 1960s when the government had stabilized under the restored leadership of a king, action was taken against the widespread destruction of the wildlife habitat. Some of the human settlements in the Chitawan valley were removed and part of the area became a reserve; however, some poaching still went on. A helicopter census in 1968 estimated the Chitawan rhino population to be between 81 and 108 individuals. In the early 1970s this population began to show an increase. It was thought to number 210 animals by 1973, the year when the Nepalese government established the Royal Chitawan National Park, covering 546 square kilometres. With the help of several international organizations, including the World Wildlife Fund and the Fauna Preservation Society, adequate manpower was trained and equipped to administer the park. In 1976 the Royal Nepalese Army began patrolling it, and poaching virtually stopped. The following year the park was extended to 907 square kilometres, and it is today one of the main tourist attractions of Nepal and one of the most important rhino reserves in the world.

In India, official action to conserve rhinos took place earlier. Rhino hunting was abolished in 1910, and soon afterwards state governments began to protect a few of the areas where rhinos still remained. In 1908 Kaziranga had been declared a forest reserve; it became a game sanctuary eight years later and was closed to the public until 1938. Laokhowa, 80 kilometres west of Kaziranga, was established as a forest reserve around 1929. In the neighbouring state of West Bengal, Jaldapara was unofficially recognized as a reserve in 1936 and officially became a sanctuary primarily for rhinos in 1941. Today it has West Bengal's largest rhino population.

Despite the efforts to protect rhinos and their habitats in India, poaching still continues. Kaziranga, with the world's largest Indian rhino population, has always been plagued by poachers. At the time when it was a forest reserve, one forest officer came across 40 rhino carcasses, all without horns. The poachers then were Mikirs, a tribal people living in the hills just to the south of Kaziranga.

When Kaziranga was opened to the public, poaching declined. By the late 1960s an average of eleven rhinos were killed each year. This dropped to only three per year during the 1970s when the permanent staff of the park was increased to around 200, allowing for continuous patrols in vehicles, on the backs of elephants and on foot. The 425 square kilometres of Kaziranga are divided into forty different blocks, each of which has its own camp for the forest guards who start their day looking for vultures, which may indicate a rhino carcass.

In 1968 a poacher shot dead one of the park's men and then made his escape. Immediately afterwards the highest ranking official of the park, Range Officer R.N. Sonowal, arranged for many more guns for his guards and gave them authority to shoot at poachers whenever there was a possible threat to their own lives. From 1969 to 1978 at least four poachers were killed by forest guards on their patrols at Kaziranga; several others were wounded seriously. The poachers soon realized that they really were risking their lives when they went after rhinos.

Another deterrent for the would-be poacher is that the prison sentence for killing a rhino has increased from three to six months. This doubling of the term occurred for the first time in Assam in early 1980. In years past the forest authorities have had difficulties in getting poachers convicted of their crime because the courts wanted absolute proof, with witnesses, that the accused had carried out the killing. A lone poacher caught standing by a carcass of a rhino sometimes escaped jail because the Forest Department was unable to prove that the man had personally been responsible for the animal's death. Times are changing now. Magistrates have learnt that the poachers are being paid ever higher sums for rhino horns, and that poachers come from all walks of life—not only tribal men but also Assamese and even Nepalese. Furthermore, rhinos are being killed specifically because of the increased value of horn on the black market, and not simply because the poachers are hungry and want the meat. It has taken some time for the courts to realize how things stand, but they do now agree with the park authorities that stricter measures must be taken against poaching.

Still, it is the Mikirs who are the most frequent poachers and they both shoot and trap rhinos. Shooting has certain disadvantages: to be caught in the park carrying a gun is sure to mean a prosecution which, even if it does not lead to a conviction, can be quite inconvenient. And, if a poacher does shoot a rhino, he has to be very wary of the possibility of being heard by a patrolman. Moreover, poachers do not usually own their own guns and have to make arrangements to hire one from somebody. They generally deal with farmers who have licences to possess shotguns; heavy bore rifles are impossible to obtain. Farmers demand between 200 rupees ($25) and 500 rupees ($65) from a poacher who wants to borrow a gun for two to three days. The poacher then makes his own, special heavy bullets and backs them with extra gun powder. Thus armed, he enters the park at night, when the risk of detection is least. At first light the poacher makes his way to a mud-hole favoured by rhinos, or to a recently burnt area. Forest guards regularly

Indian rhinos can be seen in many zoos in Europe and America, but recently the Indian government has put severe restrictions on the export of these animals and a breeding pair is now worth $150,000.

set fire to the tall grasses from January to March to prevent the growth of trees, which rhinos do not like. The fresh, new grasses that come up afterwards are especially palatable to rhinos, and such areas are ideal for the poacher, who can lie in ambush in the surrounding tall grass and bide his time until a rhino comes along to graze, hopefully when it is still very early in the morning.

If the poacher is lucky and kills his prey, he rushes up to it and hastily removes the horn with a knife. Although a rhino's skin is also valuable (worth $500 a kilo wholesale in South-East Asia in 1979), the poacher usually does not dare to take the extra time needed to remove it. Even if the chances of escape are good, the raw hide is very heavy to carry and must later be dried out in the open. So, the general rule for the poacher is to grab the horn and run. He makes his way out of the park as quickly as possible and heads for a nearby village to make contact with a middleman and to negotiate a quick sale.

None of the three rhinos found poached in Kaziranga between January and March 1980 had been shot. They were all killed in pits. Pit building is done at night. Two or three poachers join forces to dig a series of holes two metres deep, one and a half metres wide and four metres long. Each hole is then camouflaged with grass. The poachers check the pits only after two or three days have passed. If they have caught a rhino he is usually already dead from the exhaustion of thrashing about trying to get out. If he is still alive he is speared.

An average Indian rhino horn weighs 720 grams and in early 1980 a poacher could expect to receive 7,000 rupees ($875) for one. The wholesale value in South-East Asia and the Far East ranged in mid 1980 between $6,000 and $9,000 per kilo, a considerable rise from the $4,200 wholesale price in 1979. It is because the price keeps on going up that poaching, despite all the risks, seemed to be on the increase again in 1980. After all, an honest man working as a farm labourer or as a waiter in a Gauhati hotel would need to work three years to earn as much money as a poacher makes from a single rhino horn. The middleman who buys the horn from him sells it, with his own profit on the undertaking, to a trader who in turn transports it to a rendezvous to hand it over to another person for export. There is a whole chain of people involved, which is typical in India where syndicates operate in most illegal enterprises in order to ensure that if one person is caught by the authorities he will not identify the others. The syndicate will usually pay whatever fine is assessed and will also help support the family if an offender is sent to jail. Conversely, should an arraigned poacher give information that leads to some of his colleagues being caught, other members of the syndicate will certainly take revenge on him.

The park authorities have tried to break up poaching gangs by paying informers, but so far these people have only disclosed the names of poachers, not the more important and shadowy figures further up the chain. The poachers, for their part seem to prefer prison and the knowledge that their dependents will be cared for, than to face the penalties that the syndicate imposes on those who talk too freely.

Poachers only operate in the dry months when the rhinos are relatively easy to find. During the heavy monsoon rain in July and August, Kaziranga becomes flooded and many rhinos come out of the park to search for food, often cultivated rice and other agricultural crops. It is rather ironic that at the time of the year when rhinos wreak havoc on the farmers their lives are least at risk. The reason is that out in the open there are too many potential witnesses to the killing of a rhino and too much jealousy over the prospect of easy money from a horn.

Horn is sold legally as well as illegally in India. Forest guards in Kaziranga and Manas Sanctuary, also in Assam, are encouraged to collect horns of rhinos that have died naturally and also those pieces of horn broken off during rhino fights. In their eagerness, the rangers dig through mud wallows and dive into deep pools to retrieve such trophies. Range Officer Sonowal believes that almost all of the horns from dead animals are collected by his patrolmen. When rhino horn is received at Kaziranga headquarters it is weighed, marked and locked into a safe in Mr Sonowal's office. Later it is auctioned at Gauhati, a town 220 kilometres away, where all legally acquired rhino horn from the state of Assam is sold.

Technically, the horns from Kaziranga are offered for 'tender', which means that the Chief Conservator of Forests does not necessarily have to accept the highest offer. In practice, however, the person who bids highest gets all the horns under auction. Auctions usually take place annually and the Forest Department puts a lot of effort into organizing them.

From the 1972/3 financial year to 1979/80, 283 horns weighing a total of 205 kilos were put for tender in Gauhati by the Forest Department. The Forest Department grades the horns into three qualities according to their condition: new horns without any defects such as cracks and holes command the highest prices. From 1972/3 to 1978/9 the price for the best quality horn climbed quite gradually from $1,800 a kilo to $1,950. Then there was a sudden jump. For the 39.5 kilos offered for sale in 1979/80 the highest tender was $7,800 a kilo.

The sharp increase in price is not due to a drop in supply. In fact, the amount of horns at auctions has risen during the past decade, from seven and a half kilos in 1972/3 to a record amount of 45.5 kilos in 1978/9. This is due to the overall growth in the rhino population of Assam and to efficient collection of horns from dead animals in Kaziranga.

Most of the bidders for rhino horns at the Gauhati auctions are traders from Calcutta, but not a single one of them has tendered the highest bid since 1965/6. From that financial year until 1975/6 a Nepalese from Kathmandu bought all the horn. In 1978/9, and again in 1979/80, he was outbid by a merchant from Manipur, a small Indian state south-east of Assam.

The only other Indian state which has rhinos is West Bengal, but none of the rhino horn held by the authorities there has ever been sold. It remains in the safe-keeping of the Forest Department, except for a few horns that have been given to museums. There is not very much anyway. The rhino populations in both Jaldapara and Garumara, a tiny reserve of only eight square kilometres, are very small. In 1964 the Forest Department carried out its first official census of the rhinos in Jaldapara: a total of 72 individuals. Only two years later Juan Spillett made a census of all the major animal species in that sanctuary and estimated that the total rhino population was between 50 and 60. In 1978 another Forest Department census recorded less than half this number.

Sir Samuel Baker is shown with Hamran Arabs of the Sudan in this engraving of a rhino hunt.

Most of the deaths of rhinos in Jaldapara are attributed to poaching; the Forest Department estimates that between 1967 and 1972 some 38 rhinos were illegally killed in Jaldapara and Garumara. Officials say that one single gang is responsible for almost all of the poaching in Jaldapara, but its syndicate is so well organized that despite searches of the houses near the reserve (in which rhino horn has been discovered), not one member has been convicted of rhino poaching. This syndicate has refined its operations which are in a different league from those of the gangs of Kaziranga. When a poacher kills a rhino in Jaldapara he does not remove the horn. Instead he immediately leaves the reserve and tells another person where the rhino is. Then someone else again is sent to collect the horn. With each member playing a very limited role in the syndicate, it is an almost hopeless situation for the authorities to handle.

The number of Indian rhinos killed in the early months of 1980 was small, but it was up on the same period in 1979 to an alarming degree. This is a result of the prices paid for the horn, illegally both in West Bengal and in Assam, where the price at the legal auction was almost four times higher than a year before. In 1980 there were only 24 rhinos left in Jaldapara, a barely viable breeding group; and there were only six rhinos left in Garumara. Even in Assam, with 950 rhinos in

Kaziranga and approximately 200 in other sanctuaries, there is no complacency among the officials who fear the consequences of the very high demand for rhino horn in South-East Asia and the Far East.

II   The African Species

In 1820, before European explorers penetrated the more remote parts of Africa, black rhinos were especially abundant. There were probably around 400,000 of them, perhaps as many as a million, and they may have outnumbered the white rhinos four to one. They lived in a wide belt of territory from Mali in the west almost straight across Africa into Somalia in the east. They were also found as far north as Ethiopia and down through East Africa, Zambia, Malawi, Angola, Botswana, Mozambique and South Africa in very large numbers. The white rhino on the other hand was limited to two areas: northern Zaire, Chad, the Central African Republic, southern Sudan and Uganda; and the whole of southern Africa, including Angola, Botswana, Zimbabwe, Mozambique and South Africa. In other words, rhinos either white or black were to be found everywhere south of the Sahara except in Africa's tropical rain forests.

Most European explorers who travelled in the interior of the continent commented on the tremendous numbers of rhinos. Richard Burton, one of the first explorers of the East African hinterland, wrote in 1856 that in Tanganyika, "the black rhinoceros with a double horn is as common as the elephant". In southern Africa the early adventurers who moved up from the Cape made similar observations. Cornwallis Harris wrote in the 1830s that he had met with the white rhinoceros "in almost incredible numbers". The great hunter, Frederick Selous, believed that at this time the white rhino in the north-west of the Transvaal had increased "almost to the limit of its food supply". During a single day's march with bullock waggons Sir Andrew Smith encountered between 100 and 150 rhinos, both black and white. This idyllic situation did not last. Some 40 years later Frederick Selous noted that "thousands upon thousands of these huge creatures were killed by white hunters and natives armed with the white man's weapons, and the species [white] has become practically extinct".

The story of the massacre of the white rhinos of southern Africa is almost identical to that of the Indian rhinos. Technical improvements to fire-arms in the nineteenth century made hunting easy. The new guns were accurate and had a fire-power that made shooting big game a possibility for many who had never before hunted. Moreover, the white rhino is a docile creature; sportsmen were able to approach these animals with little danger. An additional incentive was that rhino horns sold well on the market, and Europeans as well as Africans enjoyed eating rhino meat. One Boer trader in South Africa with an eye for the main chance supplied guns to 400 natives for the sole purpose of killing rhinos.

In the nineteenth century there was no protection whatsoever for the wild animals of Africa. The idea of setting up game reserves or national parks sounded ludicrous in this land of plenty until it was almost too late. Even game laws and hunting licences seemed superfluous until the late 1880s, and by then almost all the rhinos between Salisbury and the Zambezi river had been killed. By 1900 there were probably only 50 to 100 white rhinos in South Africa.

Nor was the slaughter restricted to southern Africa—it was even greater in Ethiopia and central Sudan, where the commercial value of rhino horn had been known long before Europeans came onto the scene. The magnificent seventeenth-

35

and eighteenth-century rhino horn vessels of China were possibly made from horns imported from the Red Sea dhow ports.

Rhinos were populous in central Sudan and Ethiopia, and it is unlikely that hunting had much impact on their numbers until after 1800. It was arduous work to prepare the kind of trap that the Abyssinians used, and it led to a most cruel death for the rhino. Sir Samuel Baker, who was in the north-west of Abyssinia in the early 1860s, described in detail the making of a rhino trap. To begin, the Abyssinians dug a hole in the ground about a metre deep and half a metre in diameter next to a rhino dung heap. Into the hole they placed a flat, circular piece of wood studded with bamboo spikes which would retain the foot of an animal should it step on it. Across the top of the hole they laid a noose constructed from a very strong rope and at the end of the noose a log of wood weighing between 100 and 150 kilos was attached and buried nearby. The Abyssinians camouflaged the trap with earth and dung. The unfortunate rhino that approached would, according to habit, scratch around the dung heap and inevitably one of his feet would sink into the trap; the noose would tighten around the rhino's leg as he struggled to free himself from the bamboo spikes. In intense pain from the spikes penetrating his foot like horse-shoe nails, the rhino would jerk about furiously and pull the log out of its trench. He would usually gallop away from the spot, trailing behind him the enormous log which would catch in every bush, leaving an unmistakable trail. The next morning the hunters would have no trouble locating the miserable animal. By then he often had become entangled in an attempt to turn around. Stilled and in agony, the rhino would then have to bear the wounds inflicted by the Abyssinians' spears which, Baker said, were not sharp enough to cut through the rhino's hide without considerable difficulty. On a few occasions a thoroughly enraged rhino was able to charge his attackers, but usually he was too exhausted to do anything. Death would come as a relief to the tortured animal.

The Hamran Arabs of the Sudan went after rhinos on horseback. They would look for tracks near streams and follow them when they appeared to lead through open country. Once the rhino spotted the hunters he would gallop away. The hunters would follow until he was exhausted, then one Arab would distract him while the others closed in on him from behind and plunged their spears into him. Baker took part in a rhino hunt with Taher and Roder Sheriff, "the most renowned of all the sword-hunters of the Hamrans". Baker rode his own horse, Tetel, and declared: "I believe he never went so well as upon that day, for, although an Abyssinian horse, I had a pair of English spurs, which worked like missionaries, but with a more decided result". It was Taher who first caught sight of two rhinos and, with his sword drawn and his long hair flying wildly behind him, he led the way towards the creatures. The going was treacherous in the extreme, first over rough ground, then through clumps of mimosa trees, the branches of which were "armed with fish-hook thorns", and later over very sandy ground. The hunters galloped at full speed and lost four of their party of seven along the way. With Baker close behind the two brothers, the rhinos finally made towards a *nabuk* jungle, which was impenetrable for man and mount. To give encouragement to Taher to try to get at the rhinos before they entered the jungle, Baker shouted at him to move forward faster:

> Away he went—he was close to the very heels of the beasts; but his horse could do no more than his present pace; still he gained upon the nearest; he leaned forward with his sword ready for the blow—another moment, and the jungle would be reached! One effort more, and the sword flashed in the sunshine. . . his blow. . . marvelously delivered at an extremely long reach, as he was nearly out of the saddle when he sprang forward to enable the blade to obtain a cut at the last moment.

The Indian rhino has only one horn, and it is usually very short. Because Indian rhino horn is so much smaller than that from either of the African species, many Asians believe that its curative powers are more concentrated and they will pay up to 15 times as much for it.

On following pages Meru is the only national park or reserve in East Africa where there are white rhinos, and these are guarded night and day by armed rangers.

Completely at ease in water, the Indian rhino may spend several hours at a time immersed, cooling off and getting relief from flies. The Indian rhino is probably the best swimmer of the five extant rhino species and has been known to cross the Brahmaputra river.

Taher only managed to make a gash about a foot long upon the rhino's hind-quarters and the rhino disappeared into the jungle, but Baker was not at all disappointed:

> Although we had failed, I never enjoyed a hunt so much either before or since; it was a *magnificent* run, and still more magnificent was the idea that a man, with no weapon but a sword, could attack and generally vanquish every huge animal of creation. I felt inclined to discard all my rifles, and to adopt a sabre . . .

That the Hamran Arabs were generally successful in their rhino hunts is evident from the number of rhino horns exported from Ethiopia and Sudan. At the end of the nineteenth century the Somali ports of Mogadishu, Merca and Brava were annually shipping out hundreds of horns, most of which came from Ethiopia and Sudan. One European from the British legation in Addis Ababa, P. P. C. Zaphiro, wrote that the even smaller town of Lugh exported "1,000 or more horns in 1905/6", and estimated that 1,200 horns were exported from Borana, the southern part of Ethiopia, in 1907. By the time of World War I rhinos were rare indeed, and by the late 1970s it was thought that they were all but extinct in central Sudan and Ethiopia. Steve Stephenson told me that when he was wildlife adviser to the Ethiopian government from 1975 to 1978 he looked carefully for rhinos but did not find even one. He did, however, hear that someone had seen rhino tracks in the Omo valley, in the extreme south-west of Ethiopia.

One of the most intense periods of rhino slaughter took place between 1927 and 1931 in French Equatorial Africa, around Lake Chad. Marcus Daly, who wrote *Big Game Hunting and Adventure : 1897–1936*, was shocked by the French hunters who armed local gangs with cap-and-powder guns and with more modern rifles and set out for months at a time in order to kill as many white rhinos as possible and to make fortunes from selling the horn. Some of the Frenchmen's gangs consisted of as many as fifty armed Africans and would return "with anything between half a ton and three tons of horns". Considering that a ton of white rhino horn represents the death of approximately 300 animals and that there were "many dozens of such parties actively engaged in different parts of the country", Daly's estimate that "there must have been well over 10,000 white rhinos shot" does not appear to be exaggerated.

Daly noted that the natural habitat of these rhinos was the open bush country, where the hunters would find them in small groups of up to a dozen and shoot the lot. As a result of the massacres, many rhinos took to the great *matteti* reeds, but they were only in safe cover there during the wet season, for the Frenchmen set huge fires in the reeds at other times of the year, driving the rhinos out by the hundreds for massive slaughter. Daly believed that the surviving rhinos changed their habits entirely by moving into the thickest jungle areas, "where this class of hunter dare not follow".

Only very few scientists have ever seen the desert black rhinos of South West Africa. In 1981 only 57 were still alive; at least six were killed for their horns in that year alone. Their rocky habitat affords little shade, hardly any water and only sparse vegetation; these rhinos consequently travel vast distances in search of food.

Partly because Victorian sensibilities were outraged by missionary tales of the slave trade, colonialism quickly followed the wake of exploration in East Africa; the law and order subsequently imposed upon Uganda, Kenya and Tanzania did not encourage the type of hunting that was practiced elsewhere in Africa. In general, wildlife continued to hold its own during the first half of the twentieth century. There was, however, one startling exception to this rule: J.A. Hunter's record of having killed in one area more rhinos than any other man has ever claimed to have shot in an entire lifetime. Unbelievable as it may seem today, the colonial game department of Kenya employed Hunter to rid the land of all rhino in Makueni, Machakos District, south-east of Nairobi. From 29 August to 28 November 1944 Hunter shot 165 rhinos, 15 elephants and three buffaloes. Between 29 June and 31 December 1945 he killed 221 more rhinos, and from the beginning of the following year until 31 October 1946 he shot a further 610 rhinos.

The 996 rhinos were killed so that 50,000 acres of Kamba country could be opened up for agricultural development. Hunter queried in his autobiography:

> Is it worth killing off these strange and marvellous animals [rhinos] just to clear a few more acres for a people that are ever on the increase? I don't know. But I know this. The time will come when there is no more land to be cleared. What will be done then?

The agricultural plan for Makueni was ill-conceived and impossible to carry out. The land was poor, the rains infrequent and undependable. Rhinos thrived in this harsh environment, but crops could not. The Kambas, an agricultural people, were much more aware of this than the government officers who tried to force them to plant cash crops and invested about $750,000 in the project over fourteen years. In the end only a few subsistence crops were ever grown there, and the whole scheme was an unmitigated failure.

Yet, on the whole, the wildlife of East Africa remained reasonably secure during the 1950s and early 1960s, despite a human population growth of two and a half per cent per annum. Hunting safaris were allowed, but the cost of outfitting one was so high that many visitors began to opt instead for photographic safaris, first popularized by Martin and Osa Johnson in the 1920s. Where big game was concerned, no overseas visitor could hunt unless accompanied by a registered professional hunter.

There had, in fact, been a hue and cry for national parks in East Africa since the early part of the century. They probably would have come into existence earlier than they did, had it not been for the two World Wars. Kenya, at any rate, led the way in their formation, thanks to the dauntless efforts of Mervyn Cowie who battled governors and governments for the creation of Nairobi Park which he used as a "shop-window for other sanctuary proposals". In an interview before his retirement as Director of Kenya National Parks on 31 March 1966, he said:

> We bumped regulations quickly through the ministries concerned and established a National Parks Fund of £125,000 development money. It helped set up roads, small lodges, and purchased some equipment. Meanwhile, I copied every idea in Stevenson-Hamilton's book, *South African Eden* [the author was the Director of Kruger Park for more than twenty years], and went to the United States to draw on the fund of experience there ... The common complaint from Kenyan farmers was that the Park laws were so strict, you could not even go into the area and blow your nose.

It was not only the farmers who protested about Nairobi Park; there were Somali tribesmen who used the area for grazing their cattle, and there was an irate horse-riding community that used the forested section of the park for their morning and evening rides. The horse-riders' representative, a formidable woman, went to the Governor's office to protest and thumped his desk with her fists until the inkwell jumped out of its socket—but to no avail. Even her petition to the Queen was rejected.

The time for national parks in East Africa had indeed come and, during Mervyn's Cowie's directorship, Tsavo, Aberdares, Mount Kenya and Nakuru were also gazetted. Then, in the early 1950s, Uganda and Tanzania followed suit with their own national park systems. Many of the major areas where the prospects were good for game became parks and reserves under European wardens who generally kept poachers at bay.

Uganda boasted three magnificent parks and a dozen reserves and sanctuaries by the 1960s. Of the latter there were four established in West Nile Province for the protection of white rhinos. The gross tourist revenue from Uganda's parks was estimated at $1,879 per square kilometre for 1970, one of the highest returns for any country in Africa. Moreover, poaching was not a serious problem. On the contrary, reduction cropping was believed to be a necessary conservation strategy: in Murchison Falls Park, Ian Parker culled 2,000 elephants and 3,000 hippos between 1965 and 1967 because of the damage they were causing to the vegetation. There were simply too many animals for the habitat to support.

But the halcyon days when game was so plentiful were numbered. In the early 1970s a serious drought brought disaster to many parts of Kenya and Tanzania. In Tsavo, where there had also been talk of "too many elephants", rhinos starved by the hundreds because during the previous fifteen years the elephants had demolished many of the commiphora trees which encouraged the growth of lower bush so favourable to rhinos. Open grasslands superseded much of the woodland; when the drought came, the elephants, in need of more protein than the parched grass could supply, competed with the rhinos for the remaining bush. Neither the elephants nor the rhinos would give way. The fate of the elephants is well known since journalists from all over the world cashed in on the tragedy. But rhinos were also severely affected, as were dikdiks and lesser kudus and other animals dependent upon bush and thicket.

Some conservationists blamed the situation on lack of park management and thought that the worst aspects could have been averted had the elephants been culled. At least the transition from woodland into grassland would not have been so dramatic or sudden. Others saw what happened as a sort of 'act of God', regarding the terrible loss of animal life as 'Nature's way' of cutting down the rhino and elephant populations without man's interference. The controversy that ensued to some extent diverted attention from the even more serious threat to wildlife posed by developments in Uganda at that time.

The coup d'état which brought in Idi Amin as Uganda's head of state in 1971 led to a breakdown in law and order throughout the country; many of the most able people in the game and national parks departments left their jobs, and corrupt and incompetent men took their places. Furthermore, Uganda's monetary economy collapsed, and this encouraged smuggling of both coffee and ivory by those in desperate need of cash. What foreign exchange the government was able to earn through the export of coffee, tea, copper and cotton was largely spent on perks for government officials, the military and the police; the maintenance of parks and reserves held very low priority. When trucks, four-wheel-drive vehicles, airplanes and radio equipment broke down they were usually not repaired because of lack of spare parts. Poaching became more and more difficult to combat at the same time as more and more people were being forced to poach wildlife in order to avoid starvation. President Amin's men in the military, police and civil service took part in the wildlife slaughter which they regarded both as a commercial venture and as a sport.

The decline of elephants was especially severe. The elephant population of Kabalega Falls (formerly Murchison) dropped 84 per cent from 14,309 in 1973 to 2,246 in 1975. In Ruwenzori National Park (formerly Queen Elizabeth), the losses were similar: in 1973 there were 2,731 elephants; by 1975 there were only 1,047. There are no statistics for Uganda's rhino populations during these years; however, as every poacher knows, it is easier to kill a rhino than an elephant and there is big money in rhino horn. It seems certain that large numbers of rhinos must have been killed off.

In April 1979, when Idi Amin's regime collapsed after the Tanzanian invasion, thousands of his troops retreated northwards to the safety of Sudan. On their way they passed through Kabalega where they looted the park's stores and slaughtered almost any wild creature that crossed their path, including tame white rhinos that had earlier been introduced from West Nile Province. The fleeing troops still had one helicopter in working order, and this was used for the wholesale slaughter of elephant and buffalo. When word came that the Tanzanian army was not far behind, Amin's forces fled yet again with their stolen vehicles, ivory, rhino horn, meat and ammunition. They also carried along typewriters, beds and other furnishings from park lodges.

After the Ugandan troops had left Kabalega, but before the Tanzanians arrived, civilians living on the park's borders had their turn at looting. There was absolutely no control or authority over the situation; people were more or less free to pillage whatever they could until they were stopped by the Tanzanians. The Tanzanians, too, quickly realized that there was a demand for meat from game animals, so after a short break they continued the slaughter for their own profit. It is believed that more than 75 per cent of all the game in Kabalega was killed in 1979.

Farther south, in the Ruwenzori National Park, Tanzanian troops were similarly involved in large-scale massacres of wild animals for food and personal profit. An American scientist, Karl von Orsdol, witnessed the butchery:

April 27: Woken up before dawn by machine-gun fire. It turns out to be Tanzanian troops hunting for hippo. Sporadic fire through most of the morning, and the result is four hippos dead and butchered on the spot. Apparently the meat is going across Lake Edward to Zaire as well as to local markets. Several hippo have been hit, but not followed up and killed. These will slowly bleed to death . . .

April 29: The Park was left with only three vehicles by the retreating Amin forces. Then the Tanzanians commandeered one of these, returning it today with its engine wrecked. They said they needed it to supply the troops in the Park with food and water. But, as the Senior Warden pointed out to them, they'd used it to transport poached meat.

June 18: A truck arrives, open-backed and full of about fifteen Tanzanian soldiers. They go for a herd of about four hundred topi, blazing away as they crash and bump along—missing more than they hit. They keep up the chase for several miles, then slowly pick up the corpses strewn around the battlefield. They ignore the winged and wounded.

July 6: I'm told that more than fifty civilian poachers have been arrested in the past two weeks . . . The Police released all of them on orders from the Tanzanian Army.

From bows and arrows, rhino poachers in Kenya have switched to automatic weapons.

In March and April 1980 Dr Iain Douglas-Hamilton counted elephants in Uganda. He found that only 1,360 elephants remained in Kabalega National Park and that there were only 150 elephants left alive in the whole of Ruwenzori National Park. He did not see a single rhino in Kabalega and his view was that most of those in Ajai Sanctuary had also been killed. There had been under 40 black rhinos and probably 15 white in late 1979. Iain says that he would be surprised if there were more than a dozen left now in the whole of Uganda.

Ugandan wildlife faces a bleak future. Almost three years after the Tanzanian 'liberation', chaos still reigns. The national parks of the country exist in little more than name, with very limited staff and equipment; the few remaining administrators face a formidable task in trying to keep hungry people from killing game for food. It is also a point of view that when there are hardly any wild animals left aside from those in the parks in Uganda, the very idea of a game department (which in East Africa plays the role of controlling poaching outside parks and protecting people from marauding wild animals) may be obsolete today. In April 1980 the Chief Game Warden of Uganda, John Bushara, told me that his game

department did not even have one functioning vehicle. When I looked at him in dismay without replying, his eyes flashed with unspoken expletives and he added, "we don't even have a bicycle".

How can international conservation agencies help reverse such a desperate situation? Things are so dismal in Uganda that a positive answer cannot be given. Where people are suffering so grievously animals must of course take second place. International relief organizations have had to give up many attempts to alleviate the starvation of Karamajong pastoralists in the north of the country, so what hope do rhinos have? Traversing war-strewn roads and tracks from the country's capital, Red Cross, CARE and other aid groups have had their trucks ambushed by armed bandits in the course of their mercy missions.

In Kenya the human situation is far better but the prospects for rhinos are grim. In 1969 Kenya had at least 16,000 rhinos and possibly as many as 20,000; today there are under 1,500 left. The Tsavo ecosystem, which embraces Tsavo East and Tsavo West parks as well as adjacent areas, proudly used to proclaim the world's greatest populations: between 6,000 and 9,000 in 1969. The drought in 1970/1 caused the deaths of nearly 1,000 rhinos, but the fact that in 1981 there were less than 200 left alive had nothing at all to do with the weather.

The background to Kenya's tragic rhino story is quite complex.

Poaching, always more of a threat in Kenya than elsewhere in East Africa, quickly became a way of life for the Waata tribesmen (more popularly known as the Liangulu), who had small settlements in and around Tsavo at the time of the park's founding. In the past this tribe had hunted elephant for food and would camp around a carcass until they had consumed all the meat. However, by the late 1940s the Liangulus were instead illegally hunting for ivory and rhino horn which they sold through middlemen to Arab and Asian dealers in Mombasa. They had perfected their hunting skills, using very powerful bows (some bows had draw weights of more than 60 kilos). They tipped their arrows with a poison made from the *Acokanthera* tree which would quickly enter the animal's bloodstream and cause heart failure.

The most famous surviving Liangulu hunter is Galogalo Kafonde. David Sheldrick, who became warden of Tsavo East in 1949, hated Galogalo because of all his misdeeds, but one could not help but respect his wiliness. Once when Sheldrick caught him he arranged an ingenious escape, and he played cat-and-mouse with the authorities for years. He was the principal character in Dennis Holman's book, *The Elephant People*, and he played his own role in the film 'Bloody Ivory'. Recently, he talked to Ian Parker, who has known him for years, and told him the details of his 40-year poaching career. He admits to having killed several hundred rhinos. His favourite technique was to climb a tree when he saw a rhino downwind and to call the beast to him, by emitting a fair imitation of a rhino squeak. When the rhino came trotting along, Galogalo would shoot his poisoned arrow, aiming carefully for a part of the anatomy where he would be sure to hit blood vessels. The stricken rhino would fall within a few hundred yards, after which it took less than three minutes to remove the animal's horns with a sharp knife. If he were hungry, Galogalo would also cut off a hunk of meat for himself. He stored the horn, along with poached ivory, in the bush, in his own or in friends' huts, until a buyer approached him. Sometimes the accumulated trophies grew so numerous that Galogalo would himself go in search of a middleman to make a transaction. He and other Liangulus were paid between 70 cents and a dollar per half-kilo by Giriama, Duruma or Kamba agents. Occasionally they would get as much as three dollars a kilo for very fine rhino horn, but the value was always calculated by weight. The African middlemen took the trophies to the coastal towns where they doubled and sometimes tripled their prices when they re-sold them to exporters.

45

The greatest amount of horn from any one rhino that Galogalo shot was an almost incredible 22 kilos. He told Ian Parker that the rhino had two pairs of front horns, two pairs of back horns and one extra horn farther up on its head. Another oddity as far as horns are concerned came from a rhino killed by Kathuo Kagalla, an ace Giriama hunter who was one of Galogalo's peers. The rhino had a long horn which was almost translucent with a whitish cast to it. When Kathuo went to sell it, he was hijacked by some crooks posing as game scouts who stole it from him and passed it on to a dealer.

In the course of early foot safaris in the north of Tsavo East, Sheldrick discovered intensive poaching being done by Kamba tribesmen. The Kambas made effective wire snares for smaller game but they were not as adept as the Liangulus with bows and arrows; moreover, the poisons they used sometimes led to long and agonizing deaths for their victims. Some Kambas dipped their arrowheads into nitric acid which tended to neutralize the poison (rather than make it stronger). As a result, elephants and rhinos shot by the Kambas often died of septicaemia. Like the Liangulus, the Kambas sold their trophies to middlemen who took them to dealers in Mombasa and Malindi.

Sheldrick's first move against the poachers involved building outposts for his rangers. The rangers were frightened of the poachers, however, and did not dare to venture far from the outposts. Then Sheldrick established a field force, for which he recruited warriors from the Turkana, Rendille, Samburu and Orma, all nomadic peoples from the north of Kenya, who were tough and used to hardship, and who knew how to follow spoor and read the 'bush telegraph', although most of them could not read or write any language and few even spoke Swahili. Their training was on rigorous military lines, and as each one was armed, discipline had to be very strict. Still, the field force alone was not enough to eradicate poaching. Therefore in 1956, Sheldrick embarked on an ambitious anti-poaching campaign, supported by the police, the army and the game department. As a result of this two-year campaign, the Liangulu people entirely gave up hunting in Tsavo park, and the Kambas lay low. Their chances would come again, however . . .

Not long after the founding of national parks in Kenya, a rivalry developed between parks and game department people. Game department officials seemed to resent the prestige and success of the parks. After Sheldrick's anti-poaching campaign, authorities in the game department were less inclined to co-operate in later anti-poaching drives. An example of this petty-mindedness was that they refused to follow up poachers who moved just outside park boundaries and would not allow park employees honorary game warden status, thus ensuring that they could not make arrests outside the parks.

With the stated purpose of trying to co-ordinate the work of the game department with that of the national parks and reserves, the Kenya government declared an official merger of the two in 1976. The parks people were disgruntled by being absorbed into what became the Wildlife Conservation and Management Department under the Ministry of Tourism and Wildlife (in 1980 changed to the Ministry of Environment and Natural Resources). Many of them also resented having to accept cuts in their salaries (to bring them into line with civil service employment schedules). Questions of finance and management baffled even the best of government servants in the ministry, and all kinds of misunderstandings arose when office-bound bureaucrats issued directives telling those in the field how to handle matters.

Inevitably, the morale of the former parks employees fell to a low ebb. Sceptics loudly voiced their belief that the amalgamation came about because of corruption in high places. When the government summarily dismissed all honorary park wardens, who were Europeans working without payment to help with wildlife censuses and the patrolling of parks, many Kenya residents felt that the sceptics indeed had a point to make. When it later became known that private shipments of ivory and rhino horn were arriving in Frankfurt and Antwerp with licensed permits from the Ministry of Tourism and Wildlife, even though there had been a ban on private ivory exports since 1973, there was widespread condemnation of the situation. It was also noted that although Kenya had banned all hunting in 1977, and all trade in wildlife products in early 1978, those years saw huge imports of Kenyan ivory and rhino horn into other countries.

The government was sensitive to adverse comment and public criticism and thought that by transferring wardens to different parks things might improve. That misguided solution was applied in Tsavo East. David Sheldrick was moved to Nairobi as an adviser but the warden who took his place could not pilot an aircraft and therefore was unable to keep as close a watch on poaching as necessary. After a while this warden was also replaced, but the new man had no experience of anything on so large a scale as Tsavo. Poachers came out again in full force, and there was a new development: Kambas found themselves competing for the spoils with Somalis. Somalis had come into Tsavo on previous occasions, but usually had done nothing more illegal than remove the ivory from dead elephants. However, now there were differences of opinion between the Somali and Kenya governments and it seemed as if Somalis were sowing discontent wherever they could in Kenya. They invaded parks in gangs, carrying heavy rifles and even automatic weapons. In Tsavo Somalis (of both Kenyan and Somali nationality) were responsible for eliminating rhinos from several areas of the park. They found that they could sell rhino horn and ivory for very high prices to sophisticated middlemen who moved the trophies either up to Nairobi to be flown to Europe and Hong Kong, or to the coast where they arranged transport for horn and ivory by sea to other countries.

In 1977 I spent some time in the northern part of Tsavo East. Joy Adamson was looking for a suitable place to reintroduce her leopard, Penny, to the wild. She asked me to accompany her on two trips to survey this area, which the government had told her she might use for her project.

We were shocked by what we saw. Wherever we turned we found evidence of poaching: rotting elephant and rhino carcasses, all with tusks and horns removed. We talked to rangers who told us they were powerless against the superior weaponry and numbers of the Somalis. Once we made our way to the town of Mtito Andei, where we hoped for a peaceful night in the lodge. Instead, the town was seething with Somalis and Kambas, and there was a sinister eeriness of underhand dealings.

After having combed the whole of northern Tsavo East, we discussed the situation with park authorities who frankly thought it likely that Penny would be shot for her skin if released in Tsavo; Joy's own safety would also be in jeopardy, they said. Joy concluded that the park was not for her, and shortly afterwards she chose Shaba Game Reserve for Penny's release. Penny the leopard survived Joy in the wild; it was at Shaba where Joy was murdered on 3 January 1980.

By 1979 Kamba and Somali poachers had killed most of the rhinos in the 20,800 square kilometres of Tsavo East and West: the population plummeted 96 per cent in just four years. People were wondering whether any rhinos there would survive, even though at the crisis point Bill Woodley became the Warden of Tsavo West and Joseph Kioko took over Tsavo East. Both are superb managers and highly experienced; they are pilots as well and can direct anti-poaching operations from the air. However, the task facing them was formidable. Woodley immediately set out rebuilding the morale of the Tsavo Field Force. Then, on several occasions, he and Kioko called in the new national anti-poaching unit, which operates under Ted Goss and moves from park to park. Together, they took very strong measures against the poachers. They were helped also by the fact that a general clamp-down on the trade made it more difficult for poachers to sell ivory to middlemen in Nairobi. As a result of the tremendous efforts made in Tsavo, the situation has turned around—at least temporarily. However, rhino horn is in greater demand than ever before, and people somewhere are able to get it out of the country and onto international markets. While only one rhino is known to have been poached in Tsavo in the last eighteen months, Kioko and Woodley do not dare let up on their constant vigilance.

The plight of rhinos was most startling in Tsavo, but there have been parallels in other parks and reserves. Amboseli once had the most famous rhinos with the longest horns. There were about 120 rhinos in Amboseli in the mid 1950s; by 1967 there were only 55 left. Maasai 'warriors', who had been discouraged from killing lions as a part of their manhood rituals, had begun hunting rhinos instead. After they had 'blooded' their spears on an animal, they left him dead with the horns still intact. In the late 1960s the Maasai did begin to take horns from some of the twenty further rhinos they slaughtered, and they sold them to Somali middlemen who had camps on the outskirts of the reserve.

Between 1971 and 1977 the Amboseli rhino population was further reduced to just eight animals; the main cause was poaching for commercial gain. The Maasai found it a fairly easy job, for they could approach the rhinos on the edge of the swamp on foot, moving through the tall grass, completely undetected until the moment when they threw their spears—and the spears sometimes went right through a rhino's body with the tip protruding from the other side of the victim. Tanzanians armed with guns also began to appear in Amboseli during the 1970s and contributed to the destruction of the rhinos there.

The Maasai did not take kindly to the idea of Amboseli—which they regarded as part of their homeland—being gazetted a reserve. In consequence they encouraged their cattle to overgraze the main part of the swamp which was favoured by wild animals. Negotiations for turning Amboseli into a national

These white rhinos were introduced into Kenya's Meru National Park from South Africa. Although there is fossil evidence that white rhinos once occurred around Lake Turkana, they were unknown in Kenya in recent times.

park—thus preventing the Maasai from bringing their cattle into it—were long and arduous. It was not until 1977, when the Maasai agreed to an annual cash payment of over $50,000 and a piped water supply outside the borders for their cattle, that Amboseli officially became a park.

Since then, no more rhinos have been killed and the population has increased to eleven, due to the birth of three calves. Observers believe, however, that there are still not enough rhinos in Amboseli to ensure continued reproduction. The problem is that if other rhinos were moved to Amboseli then the distinctive long-horn genetic trait of Amboseli rhinos could be lost.

Prospects for the continued existence of rhinos in northern Kenya are extremely precarious. The Somali government has never set aside its claim to this part of the country and at times has actively abetted the movement of Somali nomads into Kenya. Somalia also claims the Ogaden province of Ethiopia and went to war during 1977 and 1978 to try to enforce this claim. Fighting on three fronts, the Ogaden, and Eritrea and Tigre in the north, the Ethiopians would have lost to the Somalis had it not been for the reinforcements from Cuba and the Soviet Union. With these reinforcements, however, they roundly defeated the Somalis in March 1978. Today, as a result, the Somali population is in dire straits, some eking out a miserable existence in refugee camps and others looking for pasture for their goats, camels and cattle wherever they can find it. This search takes the Somalis into Kenya, particularly to North-Eastern Province, which has a large indigenous Somali population. The incomers are usually armed and have taken to poaching for a livelihood in a very wide area including Meru, Samburu, Kora and Tsavo. They operate in the parks and reserves in gangs generally between three and ten strong, shooting rhinos solely for their horns (sold to middlemen for about $135 a kilo in 1979).

Most of the ivory and horn collected from northern Kenya by middlemen eventually reaches Mombasa where unscrupulous dealers arrange to have it smuggled out of the country in dhows, the old wooden sailing vessels that have plied the Indian Ocean for centuries. There are so many dhows that it is almost impossible to counteract their role in the illicit movement of goods. Dhows can sail into secluded, shallow inlets and pick up cargo without attracting any attention and slip quietly away to make contact with foreign ships that will take the trophies on to such ports as Dubai on the Arabian Gulf. Almost anything other than drugs can be brought into Dubai legally. Where goods go from there is not the government's concern.

The slaughter of Kenyan rhinos has been especially severe in Meru, where not only have black rhinos succumbed but also most of the white ones that were introduced into the park from South Africa. Rhinos are extremely difficult to count in areas where they have been harassed by poachers. They hide in the densest bush, and even the most experienced observers flying overhead in a light aircraft cannot always discern a rhino from the greyish-brown mass that looks like shade cast by trees. Nevertheless, it seems certain that the park's rhino population today does not much exceed 35 individuals as against as least 127 in 1976. In 1979, the Warden, Peter Jenkins, came across a very large gang of Somali poachers armed with 22 Russian and Chinese automatic weapons. It is no wonder that the rhinos are fast disappearing.

From August 1979 until May 1980 there seemed to be some hope that the Somalis were at least being held at bay in Meru, for no rhinos were poached during that period. Then in June 1980 a gang of about ten killed six more rhinos. Jenkins now says he thinks that the Somalis will continue their poaching as long as there are rhinos left alive. The risk of getting caught by the anti-poaching unit or the park's rangers is easily outweighed by the profit to be made from the sale of horn.

When the national anti-poaching unit moves into a park or reserve in the north, the Somalis have usually already moved out, having been tipped off by their informants. The damage done by the Somalis is immense: in Samburu, for instance, they have almost completely wiped out the rhinos; there are less than ten and possibly no more than two left.

In the Kora Game Reserve, where George Adamson has been rehabilitating lions since 1970, rhinos are so rare that for a time George did not think there were any remaining; however, he has recently come across the spoor of a couple of them. Knowing Kora better than most game wardens know their parks because of the many hours he spends each day tracking his lions, Adamson has also witnessed behavioural changes in some of the larger game, brought about by intensive poaching. Elephants, for example, have become particularly cunning and take care not to show themselves in the open. A while ago some game rangers on patrol were so stunned by suddenly coming across a cow elephant with her calf that they opened fire, killing the cow and maiming the calf so badly that it had to be put down.

Kora has never been free of poachers; and, when I was there in 1975, the stench from rotting rhino carcasses not far from Adamson's camp was overpowering. A ruthless slaughter had taken place: of the four rhinos killed, two were only calves. At that time the Somalis seemed determined to undermine the development of the reserve, bringing in herds of camels and goats, recklessly burning trees and terrorizing the authorities. Poaching on a large scale stops only momentarily when the anti-poaching unit comes in. There were two campaigns in Kora in 1980, but after they were over the Somalis returned. When my wife visited Kora in late June 1980 four poachers brazenly left footprints across one of the tracks leading to the Tana river minutes before Adamson passed by in his Land Rover.

In Tanzania rhino poaching also greatly increased in the 1970s. In the northern part of the country Somalis here, too, turned it into big business. Whilst Tanzanians—especially Maasai tribesmen—are responsible for most of the poaching, Somali middlemen have encouraged them by paying for trophies with Kenyan shillings (which have a higher black market value than Tanzanian shillings). The racket has become so profitable that Tanzanians themselves now vie with Somalis as middlemen.

There are areas in Tanzania where rhinos have been totally wiped out during the past decade. Olduvai Gorge, where the Leakey family has spent 50 years carrying out research on early man, still had 70 rhinos in 1966; none were left in 1979. The days are long past when Mary Leakey's Dalmatian dogs would come whimpering back to camp, having been frightened by snorting rhinos. Tarangire National Park lost almost all of its 250 rhinos to poachers in only two years, 1976 and 1977.

Wherever rhinos exist in northern Tanzania there has been extremely heavy poaching. For example, in the Ngorongoro Conservation Area, which includes the world-famous crater, the rhino population has fallen by 70 per cent since 1966, due to the presence of armed bandits and Maasai poachers who spear the animals at night. The Maasai have shown a growing interest in buying consumer goods and are increasingly raising the necessary cash by poaching. They are stealthy hunters and usually prove more than a match for the Tanzanian anti-poaching units. Furthermore, although no one will officially admit the fact, it is generally accepted that some employees in the Conservation Authority were responsible for the deaths of several rhinos in 1980 and 1981 inside the crater. If the rangers do not improve their technique, then rhinoceroses are doomed in northern Tanzania.

Tanzania lost half of its total rhino population in the 1970s. However, because poaching was most apparent in the northern part of the country where rhino numbers fell by over 80 per cent, conservationists thought that elsewhere in the country rhinos were in much better shape. The view was that the inaccessibility of

The serial numbers on these rhino horns and elephant tusks in Kenya's Tsavo East National Park show that these were victims of the massive die-off from starvation of both species which occurred between 1970 and 1972. Later, the survivors were further decimated by poachers.

central and southern Tanzania would slow down the poachers. Unfortunately, this was not the case in Ruaha National Park in central Tanzania. The rhino population there dropped from 447 in 1973 to 94 in 1977. There should therefore be cause for concern for the future of rhinos in the southern part of the country, particularly in the Selous Game Reserve where there may still be as many as 3,000 rhinos. If poachers could kill 75 per cent of the isolated Ruaha rhinos, what is to prevent them moving in on the undeveloped Selous where there is thick bush for cover, where the patrols are limited, and where the trade in horn could be facilitated by dhowmen who already sail into the Rufiji swamps to collect mangrove poles?

I believe that it is indeed necessary to take measures quickly to combat the spread of poaching to the more remote areas of Africa where there are still relatively large rhino populations. An FAO survey in 1973 estimated a minimum of 4,000 rhinos and possibly as many as 8,000 in Zambia's Luangwa valley. However, in the late 1970s local gangs of up to a dozen men armed with modern rifles were hunting for ivory and rhino horn. In an attempt to stop the problem, an independent anti-poaching unit under Phil Berry was set up. Berry believes that while rhino poaching has since been reduced by a very considerable extent within the South Luangwa National Park, the average figure of one rhino killed a day could apply elsewhere in the valley. Today there are between 1,500 and 1,800 rhinos left, and what worries Berry most of all is that only in the places where his anti-poaching unit is able to maintain a regular presence are young rhino calves now found. In an interview with Peter Jackson for the September 1981 World

Wildlife Fund monthly report, he said: "If lack of recruitment carries on like this it could well be that in the next four or five years there will be virtually no rhino left." As for the Zambian poachers, they receive less for their horns than almost anywhere else in Africa: Berry claims that buyers from Tanzania (both Tanzanians themselves and Somalis) and from Malawi pay only $25 to $36 per horn.

The Central African Republic is another country with a large rhino population. Although no count has ever been made, Dr Clive Spinage believes that there could be as many as 3,000 to 4,000. Under ex-Emperor Bokassa, there was, of course, a great deal of poaching, but that was almost entirely for ivory which hunters could sell directly or through middlemen to an ivory-trading monopoly under the name of La Couronne in the capital city—with no questions asked. The hunters had little conception of the value of rhino horn then, but that may be changing now. Crossing the eastern border into the Central African Republic, Sudanese poachers have recently made hit-and-run raids for rhino horn.

Black rhino populations in other African countries today are limited, and the lack of control in some of these will probably mean the rhinos dying out. Chad has under 20 rhinos left, Mozambique has 300, Angola 200, Ethiopia between 10 and 20, and Uganda maybe 12. There is protection for rhinos in South West Africa (with a population of 350), Rwanda (20–40), Malawi (25–50), Cameroon (150), Botswana (20) and Zimbabwe (1,400). However, in none of these countries, with the possible exceptions of Malawi and Zimbabwe, are rhino numbers increasing. Even in South Africa, where the government provides better protection for its 625 black rhinos than any other country in the world, the population increase over the past two decades has averaged less than two per cent a year.

Over the last 160 years around 95 per cent of the entire African rhino population has been lost. Even more alarming is the fact that there were twice as many African rhinos in 1970 as in 1980.

Because the cost of conservation has soared, due to a tremendous increase in fuel prices for both aircraft and vehicles, salary rises and inflation everywhere in Africa, many governments tend to look upon wildlife as an expensive luxury which they can ill afford. The matter is not helped by fast human population growth which inevitably puts pressure on areas set aside for parks and reserves. Furthermore, the international demand for rhino horn has reached unprecedented heights. Whilst the African poacher makes well under a third the amount of money that a poacher of the rarer Asian species does, the temptation to earn a living from poaching in Africa is very much greater and there is generally much less risk. Despite the remaining large populations in the Selous, the Luangwa valley and the Central African Republic, black rhinos are in severe peril.

4 · How Rhino Products are Used

Rhinoceros horn has been in demand for many centuries and by people as varied as the Ethiopians, Europeans, Arabs, Indians and Chinese. There are records of the trade to China and India going back to the beginning of the Christian era.

The Chinese have made the most beautiful masterpieces of rhino horn sculpture. It was a tradition from the Tang (618–907) to the Ching (1644–1912) dynasties for the wealthiest aristocrats to present the emperors on their birthdays with rhino horn vessels. These included cups and decorative bowls for washing paint brushes, although none were ever put to use. They were instead treasured objets d'art, depicting Taoist scenes suggesting immortality. The aristocrats who commissioned them from the finest craftsmen of the day paid fortunes for them, and they were the epitome of the highest quality of workmanship.

Some rhino horn cups from China made their way to Europe in the sixteenth and early seventeenth centuries—the Archduke Ferdinand of Tyrol and Emperor Rudolf II collected them for their 'curiosity cabinets'. The major export period for Chinese carved rhino horn vessels was, however, the nineteenth century. Cantonese craftsmen made rhino horn cornucopias with Taoist motifs for sale to Europeans. Because these are such large vessels, only African rhinos could have provided the horn for them. Soame Jenyns, who has done research on the subject, also believes that most of the rhino carvings made in the Ming and Ching dynasties, regardless of size, were from African rhinos. Since we do have documented evidence of horns from Africa coming to China even before the Ming dynasty, I tend to agree.

This rhino horn cup was carved during the Ching dynasty, but never used other than as an objet d'art by a Chinese emperor.

There are several important collections of rhino horn carvings. The oldest is in the Shosoin in Japan, where Chinese rhino horn girdles and plaques from the possessions of the eighth-century Emperor Shomu are kept. The finest Chinese rhino horn vessels I have seen are the half dozen in the National Museum of Taipei, all formerly belonging to Chinese emperors. The quality of their craftsmanship is exceptionally fine, and the colour and patina of these Ming and Ching pieces are aesthetically superb. In the West, probably the largest collection is to be found in the Beatty Library in Dublin where, among the 180 rhino horn carvings, is a brush pot decorated with figures of Immortals in a pine-tree setting. The Museum voor Land en Volkenkunde in Rotterdam has 77 cups. In the United States the Field Museum in Chicago has many cups collected by John T. Marshall in the early twentieth century, and there is a large selection of rhino horn carvings from the Ching dynasty at the Fogg Museum in Boston.

There are still Chinese rhino horn cups on the market in Europe. If a collector were to visit the antique shops, especially those dealing with Chinese works of art, in Paris, London, or even across the Atlantic in New York, he would certainly find several for sale. In May 1980 I went to some shops in Kensington, Chelsea and Mayfair in London and saw seven; however, they were not as elaborately carved as the most famous ones, although a couple had very attractive bird and grape motifs. They varied in price from $900 to $5,000, depending on quality and size. Similar cups and goblets, made mainly in the nineteenth and early twentieth centuries by German and British artisans, are also available and their retail prices today are between $280 and $650 in London antique shops.

Very simply carved rhino horn cups for detecting poison have been widely made and used in the Muslim, Hindu, Buddhist and Christian worlds, from central Africa in the West to China in the East. The belief (which to some extent exists in

Sudan and Arabia) was that if a liquid suspected to contain poison were poured into a rhino horn cup then either an effervescence of bubbles would appear or the drink would be rendered harmless by the special properties of the horn. Dr Lee Talbot, a well known American scientist, thinks that the rhino horn cups may have been partially successful in detecting some of the older poisons which were strong alkaloids that would have reacted when put into contact with the horn, which is composed of keratin and gelatine.

In Africa, the main centres for making rhino horn cups in the nineteenth century were Ethiopia and Sudan. When Sir Samuel Baker left Africa, Hussein Khalifa Pasha gave him three cups mounted on silver bases. Rhino horn cups were popular in Ethiopia well into the twentieth century. I was taken aback soon after I began this study when I went to Wilfred Thesiger's flat in London to give him a copy of a book on Oman and saw three rhino horn cups on top of a bookshelf in the hallway. He told me that when he attended Haile Selassie's coronation in Addis Ababa in 1930 he bought one of them from a street pedlar. He liked the translucence of the cup so much that when he returned to Addis three years later he bought the other two in the main market. He believes that these cups were made in Ethiopia for various princes and other members of the aristocracy.

Cups are the best known items made from rhino horn, but there are others. The Chinese used to consider the horn ideal for their "most highly esteemed ornaments" and used it for buttons, belt buckles, cross-pieces on straps, girdles, hair-pins, combs, bracelets, writing brush handles, scroll ends, paper weights, box covers, weights for curtains and talismans. There is even a reference by a Chinese poet to a currency made from rhino horn that was used inside the Palace in the Sung Dynasty (960–1279).

Rhino horn has also long been popular in Japan where it is carved into netsukes. These are toggles, a kind of fastener for a Japanese man's kimono. For centuries, netsukes have been important ornaments and the Japanese have carved them traditionally from wood, coral, ivory and rhino horn. They are often little sculptures of insects, snakes, birds, turtles, fish and mammals.

Because of the fine calibre of their workmanship, the richness of the materials used and their subject matter, Europeans collect netsukes; moreover, in recent years two Englishmen have entered the market with their own carvings of netsukes made from rhino horn. I interviewed one of them, Michael Birch, when he held an exhibition of his netsukes at Quaglino's Hotel in London, May 1980.

Michael Birch carves amber, walrus ivory, stag antlers, elephant ivory, roots, roebuck antlers, whale teeth, narwhal ivory and marine fossil plants; but he is especially attracted to rhino horn, which he buys from Sotheby's and Christie's rooms in the form of old trophies. His finished products are translucent, in colours ranging from a golden yellow to a rich brown, achieved by polishing the carved rhino horn with sand and Russian tallow, then adding a wax and cerium oxide coating. He has made ten rhino horn netsukes since 1977, and three of them were on view at his exhibition. These are all under 13 centimetres in height and quite modern in their abstract designs. One of them represented "Baku, the Eater of Bad Dreams", and was priced at $4,500.

It was not until the nineteenth century that Europeans began to use rhino horn extensively for decorative carvings. They may have copied the fashion from South Africa, where the horn was popular for sword hilts and ramrods. Certainly, by the early twentieth century butt-plates and hand-grips for the more expensive European rifles and pistols were being made from rhino horn. During the Edwardian period in England, there were quite a number of uses, including the tops of riding-crops, walking-sticks, door-handles and even the interior mountings of limousine cars. Rhino horn items can still be bought in second-hand shops. Prices for riding-crops and walking-sticks range from $230 to $650 in London

Throughout the nineteenth century until the World Depression of the 1930s, rhino horn was put to many uses in Europe. This picture is of a mortar and pestle made from it.

today, depending on the length of the horn and the quality of the carving. Polished rhino horn looks almost like amber and it is not difficult to carve. It had a prestige value, too: since rhinos were still regarded by most Europeans as exotic beasts, a dandy with something made from rhino horn could almost certainly count on attracting the attention of his peers.

The rhino horn that reached European markets in the nineteenth and early twentieth centuries came from Africa, and both European sportsmen and traditional hunters supplied it. The rhino craze in Europe peaked in the 'Roaring 20s', but when the Great Depression came, the demand for rhino horn diminished, and it has not regained its former popularity.

Within tropical Africa, few people other than the Ethiopians and Sudanese have traditionally had much use for it. In Kenya, Dorobo tribesmen made clubs out of rhino horn, and the Turkana used it for mallets to pound animal hides to make them more pliable. The Zulus in South Africa, however, have a multitude of uses for not only rhino horn but other rhino products as well. They boil pieces of the horn in water and sip the strained liquid to alleviate coughs, chest pains and snake bites. Some Zulus crush rhino horn into a powder and mix it with milk which they drink to cure asthma attacks. One Zulu said to me that he occasionally burns rhino horn and then sniffs the ash to stop nose-bleeds. Since Zulus believe that rhinos are very strong and powerful animals, some men like to keep a little piece of rhino horn in their pocket as a talisman for strength and good luck. Others think that a little ash from rhino horn rubbed into the eyebrows will help a man attract beautiful girls.

In the Transvaal, South Africa, rhino horn is still legally sold in medicine shops which also deal in a wide range of wild animal hides, skins and bones; the principal customers are Zulu who buy them for treating various diseases and for spiritual purposes.

While the Natal Parks Board has in effect stopped all retail sales of rhino products within Natal Province, the Transvaal Nature Conservation Division still allows them to be sold in Johannesburg's and Pretoria's African traditional medicine shops. These establishments, called *muti* (the Zulu word for medicine) shops, sell hundreds of different herbs, bulbs and animal products which Africans use for both medicinal and spiritual purposes. Among the animal products available are hyena, leopard and monkey skins; elephant skulls and feet; ostrich claws; hippo and lion fat; baboon menstrual blood; and vulture brains. Since Africans are generally not allowed to obtain trading licences in the major cities, most *muti* shops are owned and run by Indians (mainly Tamils), but there are some European shopkeepers. Businessmen have found the *muti* shops profitable enterprises, and their number has increased substantially during the past 30 years. However, in African townships, including Soweto, the medicine shops are generally much smaller, more expensive and less well-stocked. I found rhino products for sale in five of the ten *muti* shops I visited in Pretoria and Johannesburg. The horn is the most popular rhino product, and a customer usually buys a piece about two centimetres in length, weighing under ten grams, for less than $5. The horn is sometimes smuggled out of Natal Province, but more often it is obtained from suppliers in neighbouring countries.

Today North Yemen—a relatively unknown Arab nation with a population of under six million—is the world's major importer and consumer of rhino horn. None of the international conservation agencies, which had been decrying the decline of African rhinos for at least a decade, had any idea at all about the tremendous amount of rhino horn that North Yemen imports until I publicized the information I gathered there in 1978. This state of ignorance is easily understandable, I suppose, since the country was completely cut off from the rest of the world from 1904 until 1962, during the reigns of the last two Imams, Yahya Ben Mohamed El Din who was assassinated in an ill-fated coup but was later that year succeeded by his son, the Crown Prince Ahmed. These autocratic, reactionary religious leaders prohibited all foreign investments in North Yemen, made no distinction between their private purse and government treasury, had no legislative body and only the Maria Theresa thaler as currency. Tribal leaders and sheikhs were the local administrators and tax collectors. When Ahmed died in 1962, civil war broke out. In *Arabia Without Sultans* Fred Halliday has described North Yemen at that time:

> It was a society overwhelmed with misery. In 1962 there were only fifteen doctors—all foreigners. There were 600 hospital beds in the whole country. Over 50 per cent of the population had some kind of venereal disease; over 80 per cent were suffering from trachoma. No money at all was spent on education by the state and less than five per cent of the children attended the traditional Koranic schools. There was not only no North Yemeni doctor, but there were no modern schools, no paved roads, no railways, no factories. The average per capita income was $70 a year. There was nothing romantic about it; it was a very horrible place.

The civil war was one of the most destructive Arabia has ever seen. Egyptians supported the republican faction and Saudi Arabians backed the royalists. It went on for eight years, and although technically the republicans won, the new administration became closely linked to Saudi Arabia. The damage was so great that North Yemen soon opened its doors to any country that offered economic aid. In the early 1970s the main sources were the Soviet Union, China, the USA and Saudi Arabia.

When I went to North Yemen, I found that the people were actively engaged in improving their standards of education, health and general prosperity. Saudi money was most evident in government-sponsored projects, and Saudi influence was prevalent in all the cities. Moreover, by the early 1970s Saudi Arabia was employing large numbers of migrant workers from North Yemen to help in the massive Saudi development programme. As a conservative, traditionally-orientated people, generally very hard-working, the Yemenis ideally suited Saudi Arabia's needs. Thus, in 1978, over a third of the adult male population of North Yemen was in Saudi Arabia working primarily on construction projects, road building and transport. All these labourers send money back to their families and the figures are staggering: the migrant work force was remitting over three million dollars a day in the late 1970s.

As a result of all this, North Yemen has become an astonishing consumer society. In the financial year 1976/7 the country exported $11,222,220 worth of goods but its imports amounted to $674,511,000—surely a unique set of statistics. In small shops one finds imported frozen chickens from Italy, French processed cheese, bottled drinking water from the United Arab Emirates, and there must be more cassette shops per square metre in Sanaa than in California! Recorded Egyptian singers wail loudly on every street corner, in most coffee shops and from cassettes installed in motor vehicles. Japanese-bottled Coca Cola is everywhere, and so are Suzuki motor scooters, screeching their brakes and equipped with jarring horns.

Some of the money earned by the migrant workers is also used to indulge in luxuries that were once the exclusive prerogatives of the elite ruling-class: qat and rhino horn daggers. Both of these cost a great deal of money; however, many Yemenis today can afford them. Yemenis do not hoard their savings: they spend whatever they can buying the things they want. Qat and rhino horn daggers head their list of priorities.

Qat (*Catha edulis*), indigenous to Ethiopia, was probably first brought into North Yemen as early as the fifteenth century. It is a bushy plant with succulent leaves which are chewed as a stimulant. Not long ago only a few Yemenis could afford to buy qat and not very many agriculturalists grew it because the market was

Female black rhinos are usually not solitary; most of their lives are spent with current offspring or in the company of an older daughter. Other than for the odd bristle, the only hair on the black rhino is on the animal's eyelashes, at the end of its tail and on the fringes of its ears. The ears are in almost continual motion, even when the animal is asleep.

On following pages In tropical Africa, poachers take only the horns of the rhinos they kill, leaving the rest of the carcass to rot. However, in Asia, almost every part of the rhino is highly valued – the toes, the skin, the stomach, the bones and even the dung of the animal serve medicinal purposes.

When trotting or galloping, the tail of the black rhino is invariably held away from the hind legs. Frequent dust baths cause black rhinos to take on the colour of the ground where they live. This rhino in Amboseli typically matches its surroundings.

Rhino hide is so thick that scavengers are unable to break through it easily, and in this instance were only able to take flesh from where humans had removed a strip of hide from the carcass.

Opposite It is very easy to remove the horns from a rhino. They are not fixed to central cores of bone on the skull, like those of cattle and antelope, but instead are attached to thick skin. African rhinos use their horns mainly for clubbing rather than goring. They occasionally break off near the base and grow back.

On following pages A bush fire reveals the remains of a poached rhino in Kenya's Meru Park.

Having found a dead rhino in a Kenya park, armed rangers examine the carcass to determine the cause of death and immediately remove the horns to prevent poachers from taking them.

By the end of the nineteenth century there were no white rhinos left in Zimbabwe. In 1961 surplus stock from Natal, South Africa, was introduced and has flourished. Those in Lake Kyle National Park, shown here, are tame and easily approachable on horseback.

To their detriment, and despite their size, white rhinos are tame and docile, permitting easy approach by man.

so limited. However, after World War II, and the expansion of the port of Aden, South Yemen became a booming market for qat from North Yemen. Production of qat as an export quickly began to rival coffee, North Yemen's major foreign-exchange earner. Qat provided a quicker and more lucrative return on investment, and farmers found it easy to turn their coffee plantations into qat-growing areas. The export of coffee fell from 12,000 tons a year in 1945 to 5,000 tons by the time of the civil war. In 1976/7 the country was producing only 3,400 tons of coffee annually. Then Yemeni migrant workers started to earn high salaries in Saudi Arabia and at the same time difficulties arose between the governments of North and South Yemen. Exports fell but the North Yemeni farmers were adequately compensated by the growth of the local market.

My first impression on arrival in Sanaa was that the North Yemenis followed the Mediterranean custom of a long siesta after lunch until the early evening; there were few people in the streets during these hours and the shops were closed then. However, it did not take me long to discover that almost the entire male population was not sleeping but instead was busy qat-chewing in the afternoons. In the privacy of their homes, many women also chew qat.

I asked dozens of Yemenis why qat was so popular; they all gave me the same answer: qat creates an ecstatic feeling of well-being. The drug is not hallucinogenic, but the 'high' it gives to the nervous system lasts for several hours and provides a tremendous burst of energy. One political scientist studying in Sanaa told me that he would often spend afternoons chewing qat with his informants, and by six or seven o'clock he would be so stimulated that he could return to his own house and work on his thesis until two or three in the morning, without feeling at all tired.

Yemenis usually enjoy a big meal at night with their families, but their earlier qat-chewing prevents them from going to sleep as soon as they would like to afterwards. Although North Yemen is a strict Muslim country and adheres to most of the Prophet's teachings, quite a number of Yemenis have recently discovered that whisky is a good antidote to the effects of qat. It is against the law to drink liquor in North Yemen; some of the hotels will serve alcohol to their guests, but this is not openly done. The Yemenis, however, have found another means of getting liquor—smuggling it by dhow into the port of Mocha from near-by Djibouti.

The romance of the Indian Ocean dhow trade hooked me on dhows some seventeen years ago, with what Elspeth Huxley called a "beaver's assiduity", and I could hardly wait to visit Mocha. The experience was something of a let-down. I was held in an office of the port for three hours, had my papers confiscated and was scrutinized by Security Forces (separate from the Police who later had their turn with me, too). After receiving permission to look around, I was tailed by two thugs belonging to the entourage of the Chief of Security. Finally I was arrested when I took some innocent photographs of bananas being off-loaded from a *zarouk* (dhow). I learnt very little.

All this whetted my appetite, so when I left North Yemen, I routed my air ticket back to Nairobi via Djibouti. I spent hours on end at the Bureau Statistique at the Capitainerie, with Chryssee translating for me. The only written information on the trade between North Yemen and Djibouti pertained to clay water-jugs from Mocha and the occasional second-hand car.

Conversations with bank managers, directors of import/export firms and dhowmen were much more rewarding. Djibouti earns a lot of money from 'in transit' tariffs, and whisky is one of the most profitable of the 'in transit' goods. It is well known that liquor cannot legally enter North Yemen and that political pressure from not only the Yemeni government but also Saudi Arabia would hamper the continuity of the trade from Djibouti were the statistics published. So the statistics are classified, but behind the classification, big business is going on. In just twelve months one firm imported $8,000,000 worth of a single brand of whisky for re-export to Mocha. It is Yemeni dhowmen who transport the illegal 'hooch' to Mocha; Djibouti people are not at all involved in this aspect of the trade. The number of dhows plying between North Yemen and Djibouti increased from 366 in 1973 to 1,856 in 1976. This is the greatest increase in international dhow trade anywhere in the world in recent years.

I travelled around North Yemen by Land Cruiser. Every day at 2 pm my driver would start looking in roadside stalls for the best bunch of qat he could afford. Sometimes he haggled with the little boys for a quarter of an hour, inspecting the qat leaf by leaf, only to turn away in disgust at the quality offered for the price. After four or five stops, he finally made up his mind as to what seemed like the best deal, and usually paid the equivalent of about $7. For the next three hours, as he drove along the roads built by Americans, Russians or Chinese, he chewed the qat on the left side of his mouth and his face looked to me like that of an extraordinarily active chipmunk. Every now and then he would spit out part of the wad and add some more leaves that he first rolled into another little ball.

Yemeni men usually retire to a special room in their house, the *mafraj*, for chewing qat in the afternoons. They lounge about on cushions, sip tea, smoke water-pipes and converse animatedly with the friends they have invited to join them for the session. Some pay as much as $25 for a bunch of qat that will suffice for one person's use in an afternoon. The best qat is freshly picked, and lorries rush it to city centres every morning.

The importance, economically and socially, of qat-chewing in North Yemen cannot be overestimated. Yemeni men spent around $5 a day each on qat in 1978; for many this represented a very considerable portion of their income. Little business is carried on in the afternoons, and the working day is practically halved because of qat-chewing. Not only is coffee being uprooted for qat, but also the basic staple foods of the Yemenis—millet, sorghum and wheat—have given away to qat cultivation. Diets are rapidly changing to imported tinned and processed foods. Anthropologists studying the culture of the Yemenis are also noting significant changes in life-style due to the prevalence of qat. The close bonds between the men and their wives are breaking down in some instances because the women are distressed by the impotence of their husbands which they believe is directly related to excessive use of qat. Another sore point for the women is that men spend so much of their income on qat that they have little left over for improvement to their houses. Yemeni architecture is the finest in the Arabian peninsula, and Yemenis traditionally take great pride in their homes. Modernization, in the form of proper kitchens and bathrooms, was popular in the early days of the new-found wealth, but the demand for qat seems now to outweigh everything else, with the possible exception of owning a rhino horn dagger.

Yemeni men almost always wear their daggers, unlike other Arabs; furthermore, they do not consider them simply as ornaments: they make use of them as offensive weapons and as deterrents to personal attack. When I went to Saadah, the most important city north of the capital, a friend of mine had asked me to look up an American nurse who was working in the hospital there. I had to wait some time before she emerged from the operating-theatre, looking very weary. The previous night she had assisted in an operation on a man who had been stabbed in the back by a fellow Yemeni wielding his dagger. Afterwards she had helped with the intricate work of saving another man's hand that had been almost completely severed by a dagger. Apparently he had had a "minor quarrel" with his neighbour. Two serious operations in less than 24 hours due to dagger wounds was certainly above the norm; nevertheless, the nurse said that dagger-fights were one of the main causes of admissions to the hospital's casualty department. "Don't think for a moment that a Yemeni will hesitate to use his dagger if he is provoked", she cautioned. At Sam City Hotel (the only so-called international standard hotel in Sanaa in 1978), men were politely requested to leave their daggers at the front desk when they came in for tea. Some became infuriated and stalked away, rather than give up their weapons.

When a boy reaches the age of 11 or 12, he is considered a man and must have his own dagger, which the Yemenis call a *djambia*. His father may give him one that belonged to another member of the family or go to the souk to buy a new one. The souk in Sanaa is the most famous in North Yemen; it is a large, walled market, packed with shops and stalls, and people from all over the country come here to do their most important shopping. The ingredients make this one of the world's most colourful markets: women sheathed in multi-coloured veils, carrying buckets or baskets on their heads; turbaned men in gathered skirts and ornate dagger belts; donkeys in every shade from pitch black to white with woven red halters and brass trappings; motor scooters adorned with plastic flowers; tiny trucks overflowing with passengers and goods; Land Rovers bullying their way through the crowds in narrow twisting alleys; and a background of eighteenth-century stone houses rising seven and eight stories high with alabaster windows and decorated in multi-patterned white plaster designs.

It is here where almost all the rhino horn handles for *djambias* are made. I talked to craftsmen working on handles in five different stalls; most of them were carving rhino horn, but they also used cow horn for the cheaper daggers. They decorated some of them with gold and silver coins which they nailed into the horn. They also did some filigree work on the handles, but it was not very good and that surprised me, having seen some exquisite antique silver jewellery from Yemen. I was told that the Arabs were not traditionally jewellers; they had depended on the Jews to make their ornaments until the early 1950s when the great majority of them left North Yemen en masse for Israel. Arab artisans try to imitate their work, but they are not very skilled. On the other hand, they can rapidly carve three handles from one rhino horn, and they say they cannot keep up with the demand for these; with the seven-fold rise in per capita income, this is to be expected. In the Sanaa souk some rhino horn daggers sell for as much as $12,000, although apparently a simple one can be purchased for about $500.

From 1971 to 1978 North Yemen was importing about three tons of rhino horn a year, which was three times more than the amount taken by Japan, then the world's second largest rhino horn importer. From 1969/70 to 1976/7 the total amount of rhino horn legally entering North Yemen was 22.5 tons, which represents the death of approximately 7,800 rhinos. Nonetheless, with 50,000 young Yemeni men coming of age every year, this could satisfy only 17 per cent of the potential market. There is no reason to expect a decline in the demand for rhino horn daggers in North Yemen in the near future. On the contrary, if the price of the horn were to double, Yemenis would still buy it.

There is a view that Yemenis value rhino horn daggers over all others because of some sexual myth about the rhino—perhaps that because the rhino is an aggressive animal, it is thought to be particularly virile, and this attribute is believed to be passed on to the person who possesses a rhino horn dagger. I doubt that Yemenis think this way. I think that they quite simply like the look and feel of polished rhino horn. There is also social status in the fact that such daggers, like qat, could only be purchased by the aristocracy in the past.

Although the recent mass-production of rhino horn daggers has had an enormous impact on market supply, this phenomenon accounts for less than half of the rhino horn used in the world today. People in the Far East have traditionally believed that rhino horn has unique properties that can cure maladies, and even now some 60 per cent of all rhino horn sold is used for medicines.

The famous Chinese pharmacist, Li Shih Chen, who wrote the *Pen Ts'ao Kang Mu* in the sixteenth century, stated that the main diseases and disabilities for which rhino horn could be used as a treatment were snake-bites, "devil-possession", hallucinations, typhoid, headache, carbuncles, boils and fever. If the horn were burnt and mixed with water, food poisoning and vomiting could also be cured. He issued a strong warning that rhino horn preparations should not be taken by pregnant women for fear of causing miscarriages. Li Shih Chen's 50-volume work, including 12,000 medicinal recipes, is considered the most outstanding study of Chinese pharmacology. It is the classic text on the uses of rhino horn, and much of the horn in use now is prescribed according to the principles outlined by Li Shih Chen.

Between August and October 1979 I interviewed pharmacists, traditional doctors, wholesalers and consumers of rhino horn in Singapore, Hong Kong, Macao, Taipei, Bangkok and Chiangmai. I wanted to find out how extensive the uses of and trade in rhino horn are today, and the World Wildlife Fund partially supported my research in South-East Asia as one aspect of their "Save the Rhino" campaign. Officers in this organization and IUCN had come to the conclusion that conservation measures alone were insufficient for their aims; financing anti-poaching operations, the day-to-day expenses of national parks, the creation of new reserves and public education projects needed to be backed by an organized programme to decrease the demand for rhino products. This could only be achieved by knowing where to put pressure on the trade. In late 1980, the World Wildlife Fund and IUCN sponsored another trip of mine to study the trade in Indonesia, Malaysia and Burma.

I had expected to find many traditional medicine shops in the cities I visited, but just how widespread they were amazed me. There are hundreds of shops selling traditional medicines spread throughout the commercial centres of South-East Asia. Neither are they tucked away in remote back streets: they are major places of business, found in upper-middle class shopping areas as well as in poor neighbourhoods. Quite a number have modern premises, with the traditional herbs and animal products displayed in attractive show-cases, brightly illuminated by fluorescent lights. More often than not, on shelves opposite or above, modern Western antibiotics, patent medicines and vitamins are displayed for sale.

Some shops have consultation rooms. Taipei's shops are the most elaborate I saw, and one in particular was striking. At its entrance there was a Mandarin-speaking parrot in a cage on a high stand to attract customers. There were three rhino horns in the shop window and inside two other large ones were on view. On one wall, above an impressive display of expensively packaged Korean ginseng, was a framed letter of appreciation to the proprietor for his extensive sales of this product. The consultation room was a formal salon, with large heavy nineteenth-century Chinese armchairs, their backs inlaid with marble, grouped together beside twin settees with maroon cushions. In the centre was a round table surrounded by several intricately carved wooden stools. On the wall opposite the doorway hung a mounted head of a very big black rhino (horns still intact), flanked on the left by an antelope head and on the right by a deer. Business was very good at this establishment; but, to my disappointment, the owner was unwilling to discuss his rhino horn sales in much detail.

The business hours in traditional medicine shops are long; in Singapore and Hong Kong the day begins around 9 am and does not end until 10 pm. The manager and his employees rarely leave during this period, taking their meals, reading their newspapers, playing cards (and, in Taiwan, watching television) when they are not occupied with their work. The atmosphere is pleasant, blessedly free from the jarring recorded music so prevalent in other types of shops in this part of the world. Traditional hospitality is offered even in the most humble of these establishments. The sales people make every effort to put their customers at ease, and often serve them hot tea. Most of the customers are women, the majority of whom are probably over 40 years old, and who usually come to do business when the shops first open in the morning, or at night, after 8:00.

Of the 152 traditional medicine shops I studied, 99 had rhino products for sale (80 per cent of which consisted of rhino horn). Whilst all the shops in Taipei dealt in rhino products, only half of the ones in Bangkok did, and here, too, it was the Chinese, not Thais, who mainly owned and managed them.

Rhino horn can be purchased without a prescription. Chinese medicine shops operate somewhat along the lines of Western pharmacies prior to the enforcement of strict drug laws. An example of this is that sick people are just as likely to consult a pharmacist as a doctor when they have a problem. When a doctor has been consulted the patient is given a prescription written in Mandarin. The patient hands this over to the pharmacist who prepares the medicine in full view, usually explaining the properties of the ingredients; the pharmacist does the same when he alone decides on a remedy. The clients prefer to watch the preparation of their medicines, and the pharmacists are fully aware of this. When a customer buys rhino horn, he usually does not purchase a powder that has already been made from it. Instead, under the direction of the pharmacist, he carefully scrutinizes the horn before scrapings are taken. Ground rhino horn powder is pale grey in colour and can easily be faked—powder made from water buffalo horn or antelope horn looks much the same. Since it is natural that the consumer wants to be certain that he is buying the real thing, pharmacists will often make the most of the occasion: they carefully take a rhino horn from a special drawer or case and ceremoniously unwrap it from cotton wool. Rhino horn is, in fact, one of the most expensive animal products for sale in traditional medicine shops, so a little pomp over the presentation is good for the morale.

Customers of the medicine shops in South-East Asia rely heavily on the knowledge and experience of the pharmacists, taking for granted their integrity. This faith seems to be well-founded. The pharmacists themselves are extremely suspicious of processed animal products, especially if these have been packaged in other countries. Several of them told me that they would not purchase tablets or tonics purported to contain rhino components because they could not be sure that the ingredients were genuine—especially now that rhino horn has risen astronomically in price.

Once the purchaser of rhino horn has agreed that the horn shown to him is of good quality, the pharmacist takes a sharp knife and scrapes a small amount from the edge of the horn. The resultant shavings are then weighed on a scale. In Singapore, Macao and Hong Kong an old-fashioned hand scale is often used, the top bar of which may be a piece of ivory or bone. In these places, the tael (corresponding to roughly 37.8 grams) is the weight by which the horn is measured. Individual purchases usually amount to a tenth or a twentieth of a tael. In Taiwan the *chien*, one-tenth of a tael, is the more common weight for pricing, and is obviously a more convenient measurement of rhino horn for retail sales. In Thailand, however, the metric system is used; and the average dose of rhino horn is between one and three grams.

When the client gets home, he removes the shavings from the paper package tied with ribbon in which the dispenser has wrapped them. He then puts the shavings in a glass and adds boiling water. When it is cool enough to sip, he gives the potion to the patient. Today, rhino horn on its own is used primarily for the purpose of reducing high fever. If the patient's condition does not improve within three to four hours, he takes a second dose.

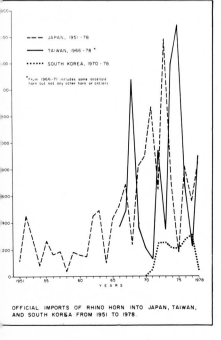

--- JAPAN, 1951-78

—— TAIWAN, 1966-78 *

••••• SOUTH KOREA, 1970-78

*From 1965-71 includes some antelope horn but not any other horn or antlers

OFFICIAL IMPORTS OF RHINO HORN INTO JAPAN, TAIWAN, AND SOUTH KOREA FROM 1951 TO 1978.

The most knowledgeable pharmacists I interviewed, apart from those in Thailand, said they preferred Indian over all other species of rhino horn. None of them gave me a good explanation for the supposed superiority of Indian rhino horn, but perhaps this was because it is difficult for a Westerner to grasp the philosophy on which so much Chinese traditional medicine is based. The pharmacists ascribed a "quality of temperature", something almost mystical, to medications. The most powerful drugs are called "hot", and the less powerful are "cold". Rhino horn belongs to the first category, but there are certain nuances of degree, and the Indian rhino is thought to be the strongest; hence its horn is the "hottest", or most potent. When I asked why, I was told that the climate where the Indian rhinos live is responsible. The Chinese of South-East Asia believe that the year-round hot, humid weather of places like Singapore is less conducive to good health than geographical regions where there are definite seasons; and, certainly, Indian rhinos in the wild are subjected to extremes in temperature, ranging from a minimum of seven degrees centigrade in winter to 38°C maximum in summer. That the Chinese in Thailand do not subscribe to this theory is probably due to their traditional familiarity with the Sumatran rhino. They may also believe that because of the smaller size of this rhino's horns, its qualities are more highly concentrated. The only African rhino horn I saw in a Thai medicine shop belonged to a very old couple living in Bangkok; they had purchased it as a curiosity many years ago—its length was greater than anything they had ever seen and they did not ever cut shavings from it.

The widespread distrust of processed medicines claiming to contain rhino horn means that the market for ready-made rhino horn powder, tablets and tonics is limited. In fact, although I asked often, I never saw a single tonic purported to be made from rhino horn except in Malaysia, where they are locally produced, very cheap and popular. The most common is called "Three Legs Brand Rhinoceros Horn Anti-Fever Water"; it is manufactured by the Wen Ken Drug Company in Johore, Malaysia. The label reads:

> This medicine is carefully prepared from the best selected Rhinoceros Horn and Anti-Fever Drugs, and under the direct supervision of Experts. This wonderful medicine acts like a charm in giving immediate relief to those suffering from: Malaria, High Temperature, Fever affecting the Heart and Four Limbs, Against Climate Giddiness, Insanity, Toothache, etc.

I came across some tablets in Hong Kong and Macao which were supposed to contain rhinoceros horn. Called "Rhinoceros and Antelope Horn Febrifugal Tablets", each box contained twelve tablets of 0.3 grams. The tablets claimed to be for "treatment of colds, fevers, headache and cough". The dosage was four tablets boiled in water every four hours. Apparently the tablets contained: "0.2 Cornu Rhinoceri Asiatici". They were manufactured by the Tsinan People's Medicine Works, Tsinan, China, and distributed by the China National Native and Animal By-Products Import and Export Corporation, Shantung Native Produce Branch, Tsingtao, China. These were very cheap, about two cents each.

I also saw other tablets containing rhino horn made in China for sale in Indonesia. These included laryngitis pills with a label which claims their contents to be: "10% rhino horn, 30% borax, 28% *Rhizoma coptidis*, 10% toadcake, 7% bear gall, 7% pearls, 5% cow-bezoar and 3% musk". The retail price for 30 such pills (minute in size) was $1.40. Another Chinese manufactured medicine containing rhino horn, which I found only in Djakarta, was "Dendrobrium Moniliforme Night Sight Pills", produced by the Tsinan People's Medicine Works once again. These pills are supposed to be dissolved in water before being taken; they are supposed to improve the eyesight of those who suffer not only

A slip of paper, like this, is generally packed with all manufactured rhino drugs exported by China to the South-East Asian market; China earns more foreign currency than any other country for its manufactured rhino horn medicines.

Some pharmaceutical firms in Malaysia manufacture anti-fever waters, allegedly containing rhino horn, as shown in this picture; the other drugs shown here are from China, and the wax ball at the front is a protective case for tablets containing rhino horn and other ingredients used as a tranquillizer.

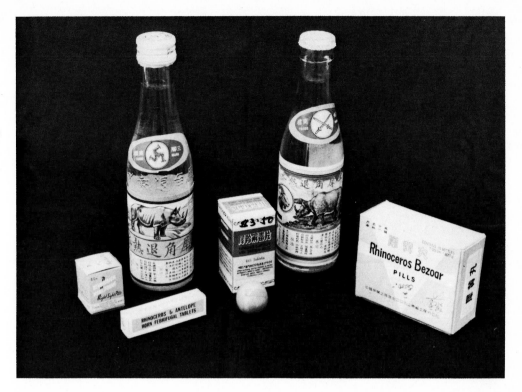

from night-blindness but also from myopia. They have in them 50% honey, 4.8% ginseng, 1.2% rhino horn and many different kinds of herbal matter. The retail price of six grams of these pills, which came enclosed in a protective wax ball, was only 83 cents.

In English versions of dozens of Chinese medicine books and from translations friends made for me of standard Chinese texts dealing with traditional medicine, I never once found rhino horn mentioned as a possible aphrodisiac. I began to suspect that, contrary to the popular view, rhino horn was never used by the Chinese as a love-potion. My thoughts were confirmed in Singapore when I visited the Chinese Physicians Association and talked with one of their foremost research officers in traditional Chinese medicine, Stephen Lau Kiew Teck. Stephen very kindly translated for me all the passages pertaining to rhino in the *Chinese Medical Dictionary*, one of the most complete Chinese reference books on traditional medicine. It contains a full description, covering several pages, of each of the five species of rhino (the accuracy of which surpasses many contemporary natural histories). Then, for each of the species, it lists the uses for the horn, skin and meat. In every case, horn is taken primarily for treating high fevers.

Because people in the West believe that the Chinese do use rhino horn as a sexual stimulant, I looked very hard for any indication of how this belief gained ground. The Chinese I talked to were not at all indignant about my enquiries, but they could offer no explanation, despite their willingness to help. In the course of extensive interviews with over 200 Chinese pharmacists, traders and doctors, I became all the more convinced that this is a completely unfounded myth created by Europeans.

It is, however, a near impossible task to try shake the belief that Westerners have regarding the Chinese and rhino horn. I gave all the results of my research in South-East Asia to a wildlife conservation agency for presentation at a conference of their highest officers. Despite this, they continued to imply in their fund-raising advertisements that there are two major uses of rhino horn—and that one of them is as an aphrodisiac. Later, I wrote a popular article on the subject of myths about rhino horn and submitted it to a magazine published for several zoological societies. The editor wrote back to me saying, "For ages, anyone who cares about wildlife has learned that powdered rhino horn is used by the Chinese as a love-potion". Moreover, one of the referees contended that "the Chinese simply don't wish to look foolish in the eyes of the Western world and thus disclaim [its] use".

In making the point that the Chinese do not consider rhino horn an aphrodisiac, I do not intend to give the impression that the Chinese do not use other products for this purpose. On the contrary, the Chinese have a multitude of aphrodisiacs and they are probably almost as common now as they have ever been. According to Chinese writings on traditional medicine, a pig's kidney may be eaten to cure impotence, and deer antlers are an "excellent excitant for men whose sexual potency is declining". Dragonflies are "counted among the love-medicines since they reputedly intensify sexual vigour". Other traditional Chinese aphrodisiacs include the brain of the monkey, the tongue of a sparrow, human placenta, the tail of the deer, the penis of a white horse, mutton from wild sheep, velvet antlers of the Sika deer, rabbit hair from old brushes, and human fingernails.

The most common aphrodisiacs from an animal that I saw for sale in the larger medicine shops in South-East Asia were tiger penises and testicles. They were all dried and usually packaged in China, but because of their low price (between $17 and $78 per set), there was some doubt as to whether they were genuine or whether they had come from other cats. Chinese men wishing to improve their sexual performance place the dried sexual parts of a male tiger into a bottle of European brandy and leave them to soak for up to six months. Then, immediately before engaging in sexual intercourse, they drink some of the brandy! Other aphrodisiacs I saw in pharmacies in South-East Asia were dried deer penises and testicles at $150, dried geckos, and snake blood mixed with snake gall-bladder.

A wide variety of animal-based aphrodisiacs can be found in 'Snake Alley', off Hwa Hsi Street in Taipei. 'Snake Alley' has become one of the major tourist attractions in Taiwan, and tour operators take busloads of foreign visitors there at night to see the sights (which include Taiwanese eating dogs in the food stalls). In order to learn something about the animal trade in Taipei, I went there one afternoon (I chose this time because I wanted to take photographs). Outside the first shop I stopped at for an interview was an eagle on a chain, perched above a carton full of live Taiwanese snakes. Inside were hundreds of bottles full of dead snakes, preserved in Chinese wines. Potions from these bottles as well as tablets made from ground up snake penises ($28 for 40 tablets) are taken by Taiwanese men as sexual stimulants. As I left the first shop, the proprietor of another one nearby was beginning to attract a large crowd. With my interpreter, an attractive young Chinese girl, I went to join the throng of men listening to the shopkeeper. With a microphone around his neck, a knife in one hand and a wriggling snake in the other, the propietor cut open the snake and drained its blood into a glass. He added some wine and then removed the gall-bladder from the snake and mixed it into the potion. After haranguing the crowd for a quarter of an hour about the value of his snake tonic, one man came forward, paid $2.25 and quickly swallowed the concoction.

Farther down 'Snake Alley', I saw a man on a motorcycle with a yellow monkey from the Taiwanese mountains, which he was offering for sale at $100. He also had in tow a bear, for which he was asking $1,050. Although passers-by were intrigued by the bear and stopped to watch it for a while, the mobile entrepreneur had no customers; I cannot imagine to what use a Taiwanese, living in a small flat with a large family, would put the bear!

Not far from this spectacle, an old man was squatting on the street corner, surrounded by stuffed monkeys, skulls of various animals and reptiles, and a stack of dried terrapins, all the while extolling the virtues of these creatures in the Taiwanese dialect to a crowd of about twenty. Across from this group were several

The Burmese Padamya Rejuvenating Powder is said to contain not only rubies and valuable minerals but also rhino blood.

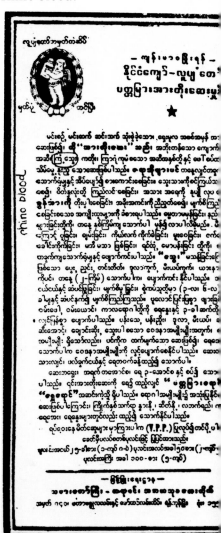

other men sitting at tables set out on the street, being served snake meat, snake blood and juices.

On my way out of 'Snake Alley', I witnessed a tortoise being gruesomely dismembered in front of a large crowd who were more interested in watching women wrestling on a colour television set just inside the merchant's shop. At the end of his performance with the tortoise, the man was unable to sell the meat and retreated to the back of his shop to give the remains to his employees.

All these activities took place in the quiet of the afternoon. At night business is much brisker, and the whole area is packed with men who come here to consume aphrodisiacs before visiting the red light district. Not surprisingly, given the fascination of the Taiwanese for animal products (and curious pets), rhino commodities are more widely available in Taipei than in any other city I visited.

Could the myth about the rhino horn being used by the Chinese as an aphrodisiac have originated from the fact that they do indeed use many odd animal products for this purpose? I doubt that. I believe it arose as a result of the trade in rhino horn from East Africa. From the 1830s until quite recent times, Indians controlled this trade, and ivory also. With an eye to markets in the Far East, they bought most of the available rhino horn—and East Africa had become the world's major supplier—from middlemen and at government auctions. Out of curiosity more than anything else, Europeans asked the Indians who bought the rhino horn and why. The Indians answered that it was mainly the Chinese and that it was an aphrodisiac, the latter point being true in certain parts of India, although most Indians make no use of rhino horn for any purpose whatsoever. But, taking at face value the answers given to them, the Europeans in East Africa perpetuated the assumption made by the traders.

The myth gained momentum in the writings of many famous people. Noel Simon mentioned the "fact" in one of the classics on Kenyan wildlife. The world-renowned Dr Louis Leakey, in a book for the National Geographic Society, stated that rhinos in Africa were "in grave danger from poachers because rhino horn commands a high price in the Far East, where it is rated as an aphrodisiac". Hugh Cott, Sc.D., D.Sc., F.R.P.S., wrote practically the same words in his book on animals in Africa. The late Professor C.W. Guggisberg categorically stated in *S.O.S. Rhino* that the Chinese belief in the powerful aphrodisiac properties of rhino horn "is the main reason for the precarious position in which the rhino family finds itself today". In 1969 the *Red Book* was published; it was to become the definitive work on wildlife in danger throughout the world, compiled by scientists who had gathered first-hand information from field research, but obviously not from Chinese rhino horn consumers: there again it is resolutely made clear that all the Asiatic rhinos suffered from excessive poaching due to the supposed aphrodisiac qualities of the horn.

It seems as if the myth from East Africa moved to Asia via the conservationists. Having heard or read that the aphrodisiac value ascribed to rhino horn was the reason why the Chinese were buying it in vast quantities from East Africa, they offered the same explanation for the poaching of Asiatic rhinos, which were even more in demand on the Chinese market.

Gujaratis and a few other groups in the north of India are practically the only people who use rhino horn as an aphrodisiac. Significantly, it was Gujarati dealers who dominated the international ivory and rhino horn trade from Uganda, Tanganyika, Zanzibar and Kenya.

In March 1980 I went to India, sponsored by the World Wildlife Fund, to investigate the use of rhino horn and other rhino products. I had already gleaned some information from discussions with conservationists and dealers on a previous trip in January 1979 when I was studying the ivory trade. However, I knew little about Indian traditional medicine and wanted to talk to practitioners of the two main schools, Unani and Ayurvedic. Indian Muslims adhere to the former, which has close links to Persian and Arabian medical theory. Hindus follow the Ayurvedic school which, unlike Unani, rarely makes use of animal products, relying more on minerals, herbs and chemicals. Both schools have their favourite aphrodisiacs, and from interviews I soon discovered that aphrodisiacs are common in most parts of the country, although the products used for this purpose vary considerably according to local customs.

Traditional medicine shops, particularly in urban areas, make a large proportion of their income from selling sexual stimulants to all classes, except the very wealthy, who seem to rely entirely on Western-style medicine. Older men are the main customers for aphrodisiacs; several confided that it was considered a terrible failing to allow ageing to impair their sexual technique or vigour. Consequently, they consumed innumerable tonics, tablets and concoctions in a state of ardent hope—rather like Western women who indulge in every new cosmetic to try to disguise the onset of middle age. Love-potions are just as prominently advertised and displayed in Indian traditional medicine shops as Revlon ranges are in American drugstores. They are not kept hidden under counters to be brought out only when a customer asks for them in a hushed voice. Once when I was in a taxi in Old Delhi, my driver passed a bus bearing a huge sign in English, reading: "Do you have sexual problems? Do you wish to have more strength and vigour?" Underneath, for the convenience of those whose answer would be yes, was the name and address of a Hakim (doctor) who would put things right.

I was interested primarily in aphrodisiacs made from animal products, so I mainly went to Unani medicine shops. The most expensive love-potion I saw was deer musk, retailing in a Bombay shop for an incredible $625 per 10 gram dose. Some of the less expensive love-potions included monkey glands, goat bile, the penis of a rabbit, a special gland from the crocodile and the bile of a whale. Most such Unani medicines are manufactured by pharmaceutical firms in Bombay, Ahmedabad and Delhi, and are packaged in the modern way with a full list of their ingredients, often written in the English language.

In Baroda, Gujarat, two of the more popular aphrodisiacs are dried worms and land slugs. The dried worms, crushed into a powder and mixed with other ingredients, are made into little pills that sell for 75¢ per 100 grams. The purchaser mashes them and mixes them with oil for external application to his penis. The slugs, being much more difficult to obtain because they are available only during the monsoon months, sell for ten times as much as the worms. They are also crushed and mixed with oil and applied in the same manner.

In West Bengal there are additional animal-based aphrodisiacs; one of the most common is made from red ants. During the monsoon when these ants move about in the open, they are caught, mashed and turned into an oily substance for application to the penis. The price for 10 grams is only 50¢. A similar type of oil is made out of leeches and sells for slightly more, 75¢. Tiger fat, at the same cost for 10 grams, is also manufactured for external use. A dried bull penis is sometimes mixed with what are reputedly strong herbs and then made into tablet form to be swallowed. The pharmacists who showed me samples of the product all said that it increased "vitality and vigour". The sand fish is one of the more expensive aphrodisiacs used in West Bengal. It is either made into an oil for external use or processed into a tablet to be taken internally. It retails for $15 per 10 grams.

Rhino horn powder is not as widely used in India as an aphrodisiac as it was in the past. There are two reasons for this: first, rhino horn has become so expensive since 1975 that it is more than most Indians can afford; this has meant that those who deal in Indian rhino products no longer want to place them on the domestic market since bigger profits can be made by smuggling them out of the country for hard currency. Secondly, the Indian government has made trade and possession of rhino products illegal without licence, and licences are difficult to obtain. In some states customs and wildlife officers have confiscated illicitly held stocks. Under the circumstances, I doubt if more than 50 kilos of rhino horn are now consumed in India each year. This is a minute quantity by comparison with North Yemen, South-East Asia and the Far East.

The main places in India where rhino horn is still used are Bombay and the state of Gujarat, which have good, long-established trading connections with East Africa. Generally, the owners of Unani shops dealing in rhino horn purchase small quantities from traders and smugglers and then grind it into powder. They mix the powdered horn with herbs which, they say, helps to make the potion more effective. Coincidentally, adulterating the horn in this way helps them to keep their expenses down.

In a medicine shop in Bombay, a pharmacist admitted to me that he mixes his rhino horn powder with herbs in a one-to-six part ratio. Even so, a kilo of this heavily diluted mixture was priced at $313. When a customer buys the standard amount of ten grams, he may mix it with honey, cream, butter or ghee before swallowing it. The average dose is two grams before breakfast and after dinner daily. In one of the main outlets for rhino horn in the Muslim Pydhoni area of Bombay, I asked a pharmacist how long it would take to sell the entire contents of his large jar of rhino horn mixture, and he replied that it would be finished within a year. Even when full, the jar probably held less than a half kilo of rhino horn.

As an aphrodisiac, rhino horn in Unani medical practice may be mixed with a variety of additives and prepared in several fashions. One of the most famous Indian Hakims, H.M. Mohsin, who lives and works in Ahmedabad, burns rhino horn and mixes its ashes with saffron and cardamom, then adds honey to make the concoction palatable. He recommends a twice-daily dose.

Although the majority of rhino horn consumed in India is for aphrodisiac purposes, some people still take it to relieve the pain caused by lumbago, polio and arthritis. There is also a long tradition of its use as a cure for haemorrhoids. The patient must sit on a chair with a large hole in it. Smoke rises up from a burning rhino horn placed underneath. I can imagine the awkwardness in implementing this treatment, and understandably it is rarely used today.

In order to attract attention to the plight of the black African rhino, a wildlife society a couple of years ago sold stickers with a picture of a rhino bearing the inscription, "My Horn is my Dilemma". True enough, but the rhino's hide is also a valuable commodity and in the past some people have slaughtered rhinos solely to obtain the skin, and not at all for the horn. Rhino hide was particularly popular for making shields. Indeed, a curious kind of rhino hide shield was made from earliest times in China to place over the back of small boats in order to deflect enemy arrows and spears. Asians, Africans and Arabs all at one time or another used rhino skin to make shields, attracted by its appearance, thickness and pliability. There may also have been in the past a magic belief about rhino hide in India which led people to think that they were better protected when using rhino hide shields. Even today Indians consider rhino hide 'lucky', and tiny strips made into rings are worn in Bombay to keep bad spirits at bay. Hide for rings retails at $1.50 in traditional medicine shops.

I have seen magnificent rhino hide shields in museums in India. The shields were made by Rajasthanis in the early eighteenth century and are painted with black lacquer and decorated along the edges with elephants and tiger-hunting scenes superimposed in gold gilt. In the middle of the shields a royal personage of Rajasthan is depicted, also in gold. The best of the Indian shields were made in Udaipur around 1720 but very attractive ones were also made in Jodhpur and Bikaner. Obviously, only the wealthiest aristocrats could afford such luxury;

however, plain rhino hide shields were used by the less well-off in Gujarat, parts of northern India, Burma, Bhutan, Nepal and Pakistan. Most likely, Indian rhinos provided the skin for the shields made in the north of the Indian subcontinent. Rajasthan, on the other hand, has not had rhinos for more than 500 years. One can only speculate on the origin of the hide for these shields, but my guess would be that it came from Africa. Despite the distances entailed, there was an extensive trade between Gujarat and East Africa, expedited by monsoon winds which reduced the sailing time to about a month. To obtain imported rhino hide from traders in bordering Gujarat would certainly have been easier, and probably cheaper, than sending out expeditions from Rajasthan to obtain Indian hide from the places where it was available.

In Ethiopia, nineteenth-century aristocrats also used rhino hide shields. However, they did not decorate them with any paint, preferring instead their natural colour. Sir Samuel Baker made this observation:

> The skin of the rhinoceros is exceedingly compact and dense. When stretched over a block and dried, it is rubbed down with sand-paper and oiled; it then becomes semi-transparent, like clouded amber, and is much esteemed by the great personages of Abyssinia for shields; these are beautifully mounted with silver, and are highly ornamental.

In order to control the towns on the mainland, the first Sultan of Zanzibar, Seyyid Said, had a string of forts along the coast, from Mogadishu to Kilwa. He brought in mercenaries from Baluchistan to garrison these forts, and they also used shields made from African rhino hide. Such shields were made in large numbers in Zanzibar where craftsmen cut the hide into half metre diameter circles which they soaked and boiled in order to mould them into the proper shape. Somalis, who also made shields from rhino hide, claimed they could make between 15 and 20 from one animal.

Rhino hide whips were popular in nineteenth-century Africa. D.D. Lyell, who hunted in Zambia in the early 1900s, claimed that they were superior to ones made from hippo hide: rhino hide is not as thick, but the grain is closer. In *Zambesi Camp Fires*, Robert Sutherland said that the most common product made from rhino hide was: "what is known as a sjambok—a long strip is worked up into the shape of a tapering stick and one crack from this on the hide of a native in need of chastisement is remembered by him for many a long day". Another nineteenth-century reference comes from W.J. Ansorge:

> The hide of rhinos and hippos is greatly valued in Africa because of the durable, one might say imperishable, whips and thongs which it provides. The hide is cut up into long narrow strips of suitable length. These are dried in the open air by being suspended vertically from the branch of a tree. The lower end of each strip is weighted with a very heavy stone.

An amusing incident occurred when I attended an international conference on African rhinos and elephants at Wankie National Park, in August 1981. During a break between the presentation of several papers deploring poaching, I went to the curio shop at the lodge where we were all staying. I returned to the conference proceedings with a sjambok which the shopkeeper had assured me was made from rhino hide. My fellow delegates looked at me in horror. Later, some of the hosts of the conference, staff of the Zimbabwe National Parks, examined it and pronounced that it was indeed rhino hide. After the conference I heard that they held a special meeting to discuss my sjambok, which was a matter of embarrassment. The hide for it turned out, fortunately, to have come from a rhino on a nearby ranch that had died of natural causes.

Today's demand for rhinoceros hide, like the demand for horn, is very large for medicinal purposes. Gujarati Hakims extract oil from rhino skin to rub on cuts, scrapes and other skin injuries. In South-East Asia, the Chinese believe that if you drink water in which rhino skin has been boiled, skin diseases, rheumatic pains and blood disorders can be cured.

In the last few years, practically all the skin in South-East Asian pharmacies has come from South Africa, usually from white rhinos, imported by traders in Singapore, Hong Kong, Macao and Taiwan. There, wholesalers process it into small strips. This procedure entails first slicing it into pieces a third of a centimetre thick, then boiling and drying the strips. The boiled strips are afterwards arranged in little packages measuring approximately two and a half centimetres by nine centimetres, and tied with red and green ribbons. The purchaser re-boils a few slices for each dose.

Processed rhino skin is cheaper than plain dried skin, and, predictably, there is some concern that the end product may not always be genuine; water buffalo hide can look very like rhino hide if treated in the same way. Another reason for the lower price of processed hide is that it is considered less 'pure'. However, processed hide is common in Hong Kong, Macao, Singapore, Indonesia, Malaysia and Taiwan where it is displayed in medicine shops in large glass bonbon jars.

Hindu physicians rarely prescribe medications made from animal products. However, George Watt in the nineteenth century noted that some of them considered boiled rhino meat mixed with ghee to be a remedy for advanced stages of typhus fever. He also said that rhino meat was recommended for people suffering from "disorders of the wind" and certain urinary problems. Indian rhino meat has furthermore been used as a cardiac stimulant and to alleviate vomiting and nose-bleeds.

In Africa people have often killed rhinos specifically for their meat, and when the Europeans came to hunt they also developed a taste for it. In South Africa it was particularly popular—both fresh and dried into biltong. William J. Burchell in *Travels in the Interior of Southern Africa* was very enthusiastic about rhino meat. He described a "nocturnal feast" for twenty-four Bushmen camped around a rhino he had shot:

In Malaysia and Burma fake rhino horns are put in display windows of traditional medicine shops to attract customers without the risk of having a real horn stolen.

> [They] were actively employed the whole night long, in broiling, eating and talking. I watched them with astonishment: it seemed that their appetite was insatiable; for no sooner had they broiled and eaten one slice of meat, than they turned to the carcass to cut another. I scarcely think they allowed themselves any time for sleep . . . The meat of the rhinoceros was excellent, and had much the taste of beef, and although the flesh of this, which was an old animal, was somewhat tough, perhaps on account of just being killed; yet that of the female, being fatter, proved exceedingly well-tasted and wholesome. The tongue would have been pronounced a dainty treat, even by an epicure.

John McCutcheon, an American cartoonist and the author of *In Africa: Hunting Adventures in Big Game Country*, asserted that: "The rhino's tongue is even more delicious to eat than ox tongue and rhino tail soup is a great luxury on any white man's table . . . The conscience of one who slays a rhino is somewhat appeased by the fact that 100 native porters will have a good square meal of wholesome meat to help build up their systems." Thomas Morgan Thomas, who travelled in South West Africa in the middle of the nineteenth century, thought that rhino meat was a good substitute for pork and recommended that it be eaten with cabbages and potatoes; he especially prized the liver and heart.

Some Indians, Thais and Burmese use rhino blood. The Gujaratis drink it as a general tonic, and some of them also mix it with ground-nut oil for external application to the penis to improve sexual performance. In Chiangmai in northern Thailand I saw some dried rhino blood for sale in a shop; the pharmacist told me he prescribed it as a blood tonic and to prevent lethargy. This pharmacist believed that it was one of the strongest medicines and, like rhino horn, should never be given to pregnant women. His price for dried rhino blood was $150 per 10 grams. Like other rhino products in Thailand, it came from the rare Sumatran rhino.

Doctors of traditional medicine in Burma prescribe rhino blood to patients also as a tonic and for lethargy. In addition, they believe it helps cure certain vitamin deficiencies. A 77-year-old doctor told me that during World War II the Japanese killed a rhino in Rangoon's zoo and that a little boy working there had collected the blood in two big buckets for him. Especially pleased to have such a large amount of this valuable commodity, the doctor had very carefully dried the contents and thought that the supply would last his lifetime. However, shortly afterwards the British bombed Rangoon with their Spitfires, and the doctor's house caught fire. His prized possession went up in flames. He told me that it was very difficult to obtain rhino blood today; consequently, many people use dried buffalo blood instead. There is, nevertheless, rhino blood still available; I learnt at a seminar I attended for traditional Burmese doctors that they are occasionally given blood from poached rhinos in return for their professional services to villagers in the hill states. In Mandalay at the Kyauctawgi pagoda I found a traditional medicine man sitting cross-legged on the floor of the long hall leading to the shrine. He had spread out in front of him an amazing assortment of plant and animal products for multitudinous cures. There were pangolin scales, tiger teeth and many bottled elixirs; among the latter I examined one with a label in Burmese reading: "Rhino Blood and Deer Horn Tonic Medicine; Please Use This Medicine". The small bottle held a dark, thick liquid which had been mixed by the medicine man himself. He said he told his customers to take a small amount at a time, mixed with milk; or, if they could afford it, some brandy, and drink a potion every other day. During festivals, when the pagoda is packed with people, he claimed he sold as many as ninety bottles of this medicine; at other times his sales averaged five or six bottles a month. I asked him how he obtained the rhino blood for it and he told me he bought it from a dealer who assures him that it comes from India.

In Chiangmai I found rhino dung for sale. In the course of a long conversation with one of the oldest traditional pharmacists there, I learnt that the faeces are collected only from a freshly-killed rhino's lower intestine; droppings on the ground are considered contaminated and are never used. People swallow minute, dried particles as a laxative. According to Gujaratis, dried rhino faeces can cure bumps on the skin when mixed with oil and applied directly to the affected area. Rhino dung, when combined with eucalyptus oil, is used as an unguent to relieve stiff necks.

Hakims obtain their supplies of rhino dung and urine from various zoos in India. However, a number of zoo authorities denied this when I asked them. Some said they prohibited their staff from selling these wastes, but in many zoos that I visited staff were busy making money on the side from rhino urine. On the other hand, Calcutta zoo officials openly admit that they sell rhino urine—they proudly told me that they made $750 from it in 1979. Hindus and Muslims, originally from Orissa, Bihar and Uttar Pradesh, as well as some Nepalese, come to the zoo to purchase rhino urine for 44¢ a litre. Every morning at 7:00 a keeper goes into the cage of a tame rhino and pours buckets of cold water over her rump to induce her to urinate into a container placed under her. Officially, the keeper is supposed to give the entire amount to the one person authorized to sell it. Rhino urine is the only animal product regularly sold in the Calcutta zoo, and the demand for it has remained roughly the same for the past five years. The Gauhati zoo in Assam also marketed rhino urine until its two tame rhinos were sold in early 1980. Gauhati urine cost more—about 80¢ for a full whisky bottle—but included a six per cent state sales tax! Most of it was bought by the Nepalese.

In the Delhi zoo the director looked aghast when I asked him his price for rhino urine and he vehemently decried the suggestion, saying that he would not allow his animals to be disturbed. Nevertheless, I sent my Sikh assistant around to the rhino enclosure to talk to the keeper who told him he sold some every week. When I later appeared, the keeper offered to sell me a full litre bottle for $3, inclusive of delivery charges to my hotel!

Having discovered that Gujaratis use most rhino products for aphrodisiac purposes, I was prepared to accept this as their major reason for buying rhino urine. Forewarned as I was, however, I was appalled when I found out that some men who have difficulties in achieving an erection soak porous leaves in rhino urine and tie them tightly with string around their penis until the desired effect takes place. Others mix two parts ground-nut oil to one part urine and dab on the mixture. A further, and different, use for rhino urine is as a cure for sore throats and coughs in Burma and India. In India some people mix it with honey and water and drink it at night before going to bed, and in the morning before breakfast.

Tradition in Burma also holds that rhino urine is a remedy for asthma, but until September 1980 it held little significance in Burmese medical practice because it is so difficult to collect. However, on 26 August 1980 the King of Nepal sent two Indian rhinos captured in the Royal Chitawan National Park to the Rangoon zoo as a gift to the people of Burma. These two rhinos, an eight-month-old male called Bhunte and a ten-month-old female, Loorie, arrived by air, attended by a Nepalese veterinarian who stayed in Rangoon until his charges had settled down in their new home. Although some Burmese and resident Indians were aware of the benefits attributed to the use of rhino urine, a demand for it that had scarcely existed before became quite considerable, thanks to information widely disseminated by the veterinarian, who emphasized that Indian rhinos produce the "best" type. He said that it was very helpful for many kinds of chest and respiratory problems and "a proven remedy to colds".

The keepers of Loorie and Bhunte learnt from the veterinarian how to collect urine in bottles and prefer to do so from Bhunte who stands quite still if one keeper thrusts bananas into his mouth while another stands behind him with a bottle at the time. Anyone may come to the zoo and ask for some urine. There is no charge, but the keepers are sometimes given a small tip for it. When someone wants a supply, the keepers stand around closely watching Bhunte and when he starts to urinate they jump into his pen, one with a bottle and the other with bananas. I saw this going on when I visited the zoo, and was told that during the monsoon rains, when people suffer more from congestion and colds, there is often a queue of patients waiting to have their bottles filled.

Demand for this particular product does not at all hinder the care given to the two young rhinos. On the contrary, the keepers seem to have greater respect for the value of these animals, and they make every effort to keep on friendly terms with Bhunte and Loorie. They like showing how they respond to being called by their names and take pride in the fact that they are in charge of them. They prepare their food and milk formula with concern for cleanliness and proper measurements. Members of the public watch the keepers at work and are impressed. Occasionally, someone will buy a bunch of bananas from one of the vendors' carts in the zoo and present it to the keepers to give to the rhinos. The rhinos are, in fact, considered very special treasures in the Rangoon zoo.

In Thailand rhino stomachs are dried, then boiled and used to cure intestinal problems. In India, sometimes a Hakim will buy an entire rhino stomach and bury it in a refuse dump for a few days. When he digs it up, it is invariably infested with worms which are then treated in a complicated process in order to obtain a very special oil that the Hakims sell as a remedy for skin diseases. Hakims also make an oil from rhino fat. I saw some in a pharmacy in Bombay; it was very thick with a light yellowish colour. Its price was $1.25 for 10 grams. I was told that people suffering from polio and other kinds of paralysis smear it on their limbs in the hope of a cure.

Thais endow almost the entire anatomy of the rhino with curative powers. Rhino parts for medicinal purposes often correspond with the diseased part of the human anatomy: rhino blood for human blood disorders; bone poultices for broken limbs; skin for skin problems, etc. Illness is associated with weakness; since the rhino is strong the belief is that its parts transmit something of their strength. In fact, the only instance I came across outside India of a rhino product being used as an aphrodisiac was in the north of Thailand where people used to buy dried penises and prepare them in the same manner as the more familiar tiger penises. Even though rhino penises are large they were not cut up for sale into pieces; people bought them whole and paid up to $1,000 for one. This was not an uncommon treatment in the 1940s and 1950s, but it is exceedingly rare today due to the scarcity of Sumatran rhinos.

In Johannesburg I met a very highly respected Indian doctor whose family owns several *muti* shops. He told me that 20 years ago he had the opportunity to buy a whole rhino carcass from a biologist and that he had sold practically every part of it. Some people had bought pieces of the skull from which they made a brew to take to prevent fainting spells. Others had wanted the hooves which they ground up and gave to children in order to try to cure lameness. One man wanted a part of the rhino's penis which he was going to grind up and mix with water to drink in hope that his own would grow larger. The rhino teeth were very much in demand to tie around the necks of children who suffered effects from malnutrition. Hairs from the rhino's tail were mixed with herbs and oil to be applied to skin diseases. After the doctor had explained a number of other uses for rhino products, some of which were the same as in Thailand, I looked up from my notes and found myself staring into the eyes of a stuffed monkey, which prompted me to ask if rhino eyes were used: "Yes, indeed", the doctor replied, "swallow one and it will improve your singing voice"!

Rhino products are in demand in a huge and heavily populated area of the world, extending from Japan in the East to Sudan in the West, and encompassing China, South Korea, Taiwan, Hong Kong, Macao, Borneo, Vietnam, Cambodia, Thailand, Malaysia, Singapore, Indonesia, Burma, India, Bhutan, Nepal and North Yemen. In most of these countries rhino products are not used as aphrodisiacs at all. Instead, the major use is for medicinal purposes, and the oldest and most extensive are those based on Chinese traditional pharmacology, in which the horn is regarded as the most important part of the animal. Many people who make use of aspirin and antibiotics also believe that rhino horn can cure common and widespread afflictions, ranging from high fevers to headaches. The people who use rhino horn for these purposes pose the greatest threat to the survival of rhinos. In the past, they were responsible for the severe decline of all three Asiatic species. Now, despite the tremendous demand for rhino horn in North Yemen, it is still those people who buy the horn as a medicine who put the greatest pressure on this animal.

One of several carved rhino horns from the Ching dynasty, this one depicts an old man in a boat.

Because of the thickness and hardness of dried rhino hide, it is ideal material for shields; this eighteenth-century one from Rajasthan, typically painted with black lacquer and gold, depicts in the centre a royal personage with the sun radiating from behind, rather like the emblem of Louis XIV. The four iron bosses were used to fix straps of embroidered cloth on the back of the shield for carrying it.

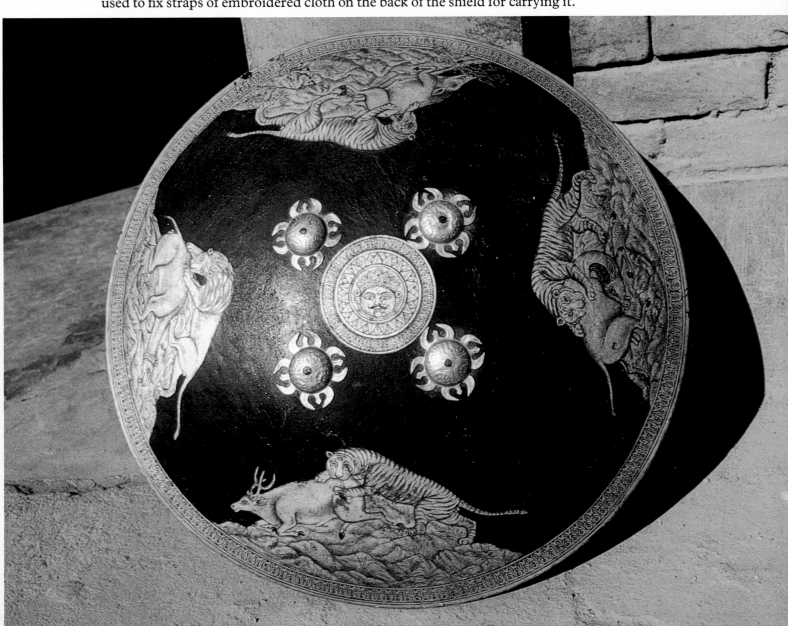

In 1971, thousands of elephants and rhinos died of starvation in Kenya's Tsavo East National Park; some of their tusks and horns are displayed here at the park's headquarters.

Wearing their own daggers, these Arabs are holding rhino horns which will be carved into dagger handles in the souk of Sanaa, the capital of North Yemen.

Opposite The Sanaa souk in North Yemen is the great market for rhino horn, prized for dagger handles.

These rhino horns stored in the Mombasa Ivory Room were among the last lots of wildlife trophies auctioned by the Kenya government in 1976.

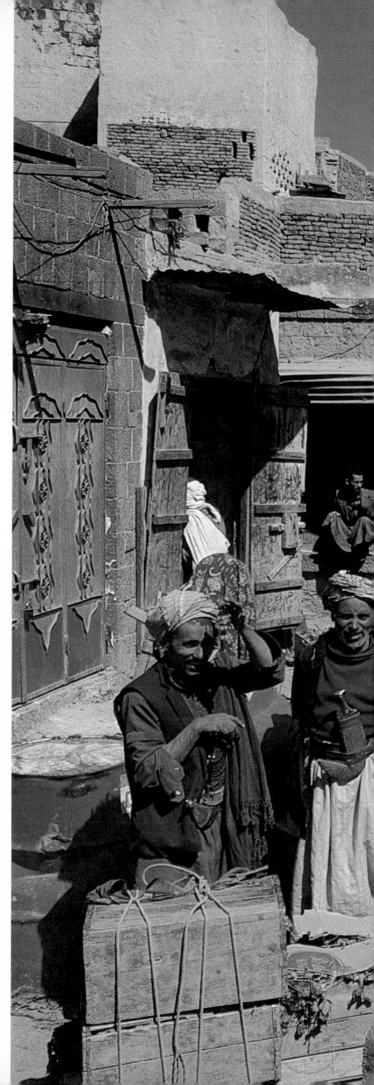

In a typical Chinese medicine shop in Djakarta, the pharmacist uses a hand scale to weigh rhino horn shavings which will be steamed in water and taken by a patient to combat high fever.

Practitioners of traditional Burmese medicine gather together annually for a seminar. At this one, held in Rangoon in 1981, they traded various homemade remedies among themselves and discussed the present shortage of rhino blood which they like to prescribe to patients suffering from lethargy.

One keeper entertains the two young Indian rhinos in the Rangoon zoo while the other expectantly waits for Bhunte, the male, to urinate into the bottle. The urine will be consumed by Burmese who suffer from asthma, tuberculosis and other chest-related infirmities.

Although less than one per cent of all the rhino horn sold today is used as an aphrodisiac, this horn, held by a Gujarati woman in the Muslim Pydhoni area of Bombay, will be ground into powder and mixed with herbs for that purpose.

In Georgetown, Malaysia, a young Chinese girl examines a piece of sun-dried rhino hide which is widely used in South-East Asia to treat various skin diseases.

5 · The Rhino Business

China was probably the world's first major importer of rhino products. In the second year AD, when Wang Mang arranged the presentation of a live rhino to the Emperor from a country "eight months' distant by sea", the animal was so rare that its arrival caused a sensation. The event was publicized as an example of how "brilliant" the Emperor must have been to have had such a tribute paid to him. Demand for rhino products had probably led to the animal's extinction in northern China by the third century BC; even in the south of the country rhinos were extemely rare by the eighth century AD. After the thirteenth century, it is most likely that they had all completely disappeared.

In the second century AD rhino horn was being exported from Ethiopia and Tanzania to Arab and Indian ports, and by the eighth century Arabs were sailing from Siraf to Canton with rhino horn. Traders had to pay a 30 per cent tax on rhino horn to the Chinese officials, but it was still a very profitable commodity. The Arabs bartered it for goods which they sold in Baghdad, Basra and other cities on their return. It took around eighteen months to complete these voyages which were, none the less, both numerous and successful—a remarkable achievement considering the enormous distances travelled by the Arabs in simple sailing craft, guided only by primitive navigational instruments.

Why were the rhino products so popular in these early days? Soame Jenyns believes that the "chief interest of the early Chinese took in the beast lay in its hide, which they used for armour plates; the use of its horn for making girdles, amulets and cups is probably a later development". There are references dating back to 600 BC of traders selling rhino hide to craftsmen to make armour "as hard as metal or stone" which was used to cover funeral vehicles and saddles. The first person to emphasize the value of rhino horn was probably the Taoist scholar, Ko Hung, who lived from AD 249 to 330. He wrote:

> The horn is a safe guide to the presence of poison; when poisonous medicines are stirred with a horn, a white foam will bubble up and no other test is necessary . . . When a man, hurt by a poisonous arrow, is on the verge of dying and his wound is slightly touched with a rhinoceros horn foam will come forth from the wound and he will feel relief. . . Neutralizing poison is accounted fully by the fact that the animal, while alive, feeds on poisonous plants and trees, provided with thorns and brambles, and shuns all smoother vegetable matter.

Later scholars elaborated on Ko Hung's list of properties attributed to rhino horn, rendering it a magical and mystical substance worthy of offerings to the Immortals. I think that this in turn led to rhino horn being carved into ornaments that became the treasured gifts to emperors. In other words, the artistic value of rhino horn followed from its acceptance as a medicine and poison-detector.

In the thirteenth century the largest rhino horns that the Chinese imported came from the north coast of Somalia. Chau Ju-Kua, who was the Inspector of Foreign Trade in Fukien, wrote in 1226 that these horns weighed over six kilos. In his massive work on the countries which supplied China with its major imports, he included a tenth-century report to the Emperor on how the Somalis captured rhinos—a method almost identical to that practiced by the Liangulus centuries later in Kenya: "a man with a bow and arrow climbs a big tree where he watches for the animal until he can shoot and kill it". According to Chau Ju-Kua, rhinos

Kenya's anti-poaching programme includes a camel patrol for use in the country's arid north where there are few roads.

were also available from Vietnam, north-eastern Sumatra, the Malay peninsula, Java and India.

Rhino horn in the Sung Dynasty (1127–1279) and later in the Ming Dynasty (1368–1644) was probably the most valuable product used by Chinese pharmacists. The Arabs, the Persians and the Indians were well aware of the importance the Chinese attached to rhino horn, and as the Chinese themselves did not venture farther west than India until the early years of the fifteenth century, they were the direct suppliers of African rhino horn to China. In fact, until modern times, there were only three Chinese expeditions to the eastern coast of Africa.

By the fifteenth century the towns along the East African seaboard had developed into major trading centres. Entrepreneurs from all over the Indian Ocean came to buy the abundant and readily available exotic commodities—ivory, slaves, gold, rhino horn, tortoise shell, leopard skins, gum copal and "dragon spittle" (the Chinese name for ambergris, which was very highly prized). The towns were indeed wealthy; Malindi, for example, used to import such luxuries as damasks, silks, satins, silver, perfume and pearls. But the rulers of these towns, Muslim Arabs, could never get along with one another; they continually quarrelled and jealously guarded their independence. As divided as they were, it is hardly surprising that the Portuguese, when they came at the end of the fifteenth century, were able to conquer them, one after another, in rapid succession. In 1505, when they sacked Mombasa, the booty was so great that it took fifteen days to load the spoils onto the awaiting Portuguese ships. For the glory of the Christian God, the Portuguese Crown and personal aggrandisement, they tried to force all non-Portuguese ships in the Indian Ocean to be registered, pay tax and abide by certain restrictions—which really meant that the Portuguese wanted a monopoly over the most lucrative trade items. The Portuguese were inefficient and capricious administrators, as James Kirkham has written in a masterly and witty archaeological study of the coast; but their presence seriously disrupted trade. Even though they were thrown out two centuries later, the old trading towns like Mombasa and Malindi never recovered their former prestige.

When Seyyid Said, the Sultan of Muscat, moved his capital to Zanzibar in 1840 and laid claim to a huge area of the mainland, stretching from Mozambique to Somalia, the coastal towns were once again colonized. However, the new conquerors were generally welcomed by their Arab cousins because, as Kirkman observes, they had no religious aspirations and their presence gave security to the pursuit of trade. Seyyid Said was himself a trader, and nearly every policy he initiated had the object of furthering commercial contacts with the world at large. He prohibited pilot charges and harbour fees throughout his domains and standardized customs by levying a flat five per cent import duty on all goods. Trade flourished once again; and, thanks to steamships, such commodities as ivory and rhino horn reached the markets in Europe and the Far East in weeks.

Seyyid Said and the sultans who succeeded him in the nineteenth century presided over a massive slaughter of rhinos never equalled either before or since. The stability of Zanzibar and the influence it exercised on the coast attracted huge numbers of immigrants from Arab countries and India who set up new businesses in existing settlements and refounded towns that had been abandoned in the previous 200 years. Each town enjoyed direct contacts with Zanzibar, the capital and main entrepot for the whole coast. Communications with the hinterland were expanded, and the caravan trade to and from the coast boomed on a scale hitherto unknown. Hunters were encouraged by middlemen to supply more and more rhino trophies which, once they reached the coast, were bought by merchants for export.

The quantities of rhino horn sold in the coastal towns were staggering. Clerks were employed by the sultans to keep records of imports and exports from various parts of the realm. From these accounts Christine Nicholls, one of the foremost Zanzibar historians, has estimated that the towns of Mafia and Bagamoyo used to receive from the interior of East Africa between 5,500 and 8,000 kilos of rhino horn per year in the 1840s. The merchants sold some of the horn directly to exporters; the rest was transshipped to their business associates in Zanzibar.

In the financial year 1863/4, according to import statistics I found in the Zanzibar Archives, Zanzibari merchants imported 6,350 kilos of rhino horn from the coastal towns. At the time this amount was worth $4,000—roughly 63¢ a kilo. By 1867/8 Bagamoyo had become Zanzibar's major source of rhino horn, supplying 9,700 kilos valued at $7,000. In 1873 Zanzibar's imports of rhino horn were still on the increase: 12,700 kilos worth $10,000 came in, making horn the eleventh most valuable import for that year. As usual, most of the horns were collected in the interior of Tanganyika, brought to Bagamoyo by caravans, and then sent by dhows to Zanzibar.

In the 1870s Mombasa began to rival Zanzibar as an entrepot for Kenya's exports. Foreign dhows and steamships came directly to pick up rhino horn, by then selling for 94¢ a kilo, and in the early years of that decade Mombasa exported an annual average of 1,590 kilos. In the 1890s, with the partition of the East African mainland into British and German "spheres of influence", Zanzibar lost its supremacy in the rhino horn trade. Exporting directly from Tanganyika, the Germans sold $7,710 worth of rhino horn in 1893, $10,280 worth in the following year, and $14,780 worth in 1895. The price averaged $1.10 in those years which means roughly 7,000 kilos in 1893, 9,000 kilos in 1894, and 13,400 kilos in 1895.

Between 1849 and 1895, I estimate that an average of 11 tons of rhino horn a year was exported from East Africa. In other words, at least 170,000 rhinos must have been killed to supply the trade during this 47-year period. The total figure sounds large, but it represents a yearly offtake of only 3,670 animals, which was likely to have been a small fraction of the total rhino population, and was probably less than a third of the number of rhinos that died from natural causes.

Where was all this East African rhino horn going in the nineteenth century? The major markets were in India (which also served as an entrepot for China and South-East Asia) and in Europe, especially Germany and Britain. In the early twentieth century Britain was buying roughly 30 per cent of all the rhino horn exported from Kenya.

By 1914 the wholesale price of rhino horn in East Africa had risen to $3.15 per kilo. By 1926 it had jumped to $11.69 a kilo and by the end of that decade it was $22.68 a kilo, but then only three tons in 1929 were exported from East Africa. Due to the Great Depression, the price wavered during the 1930s and 1940s between $7 and $8 a kilo, with about 1,500 kilos reaching world markets from Kenya, Tanzania and Uganda. It was not until the 1950s that rhino horn again fetched the price it had in 1929.

In the 1950s the bulk of East African rhino horn—around 60 per cent—went to merchants in Hong Kong. The United Kingdom bought most of the rest, although some was undoubtedly transshipped to other places in Europe, the Americas and Asia.

In the 1960s the market changed to some extent, with buyers in Aden purchasing substantial quantities of horn. About 4,000 kilos reached Aden between 1960 and 1970, but some of the horn may have gone on to North Yemen in return for qat.

From the mid 1940s until independence in 1961, Tanganyikan traders exported almost as much rhino horn as their colleagues in Kenya. However, from 1961 to 1976, official exports of Tanzanian horn showed a sharp decline, averaging 12 per cent of the Kenyan output as against 73 per cent previously. The figures hide more than they reveal. Since 1967 Tanzania has attempted to follow a socialist development strategy, one result of which has been a huge increase in all sorts of smuggling (often the only way for Tanzanians to earn the hard cash to buy consumer goods). During 1972, 1973, 1974, and 1975 a total of only 30 kilos of rhino horn legally went to international markets from Tanzania. This was practically all derived from collections made in parks and game reserves and sold by the government. We can only guess at how much horn was smuggled out of Tanzania during this period.

Because of political and economic disorder in Uganda, smuggling wildlife products from there was also common practice. The situation in Uganda was, of course, much more desperate than in Tanzania. So even despite the very much smaller numbers of Ugandan rhinos, surprisingly large quantities of poached rhino horn were smuggled into Kenya. Rhinos were all but wiped out in Uganda in the 1970s; however only 14.5 kilos of rhino horn were exported legally from the country between 1973 and 1978—representing probably not more than six dead animals.

After 1960, and probably before too, a great deal of rhino horn from Kenya was sold overseas without benefit of any kind of official permit; such sales do not appear in the government export statistics. It seems likely that by the mid 1970s, a considerable portion of illegal exports of rhino horn from Kenya originated in Tanzania and Uganda.

The front horn of the square-lipped rhino has, coincidentally, a square base, rendering it easily recognizable. Here in Zimbabwe, all rhino horns belonging to the Parks Department are marked with steel punch dies.

From 1960 to 1969 Kenya's official exports of rhino horn averaged 955 kilos a year. Between 1970 and 1976 the official trade increased to an average of 3,296 kilos yearly. During this period Hong Kong took 8,414 kilos of horn from Kenya, mainland China bought 7,154 kilos, the Yemen 4,436 kilos and Japan 1,257 kilos. Illegal exports have probably at least equalled the legal ones in recent years. Between 1960 and 1976 Asian countries imported twice as much horn from East Africa as the official export statistics from Kenya, Uganda and Tanzania showed.

Some of the legal sales of rhino horn from Kenya were made by European residents who obtained licences from the game department to shoot rhinos in hunting areas and who sold their trophies privately to dealers in Mombasa and Nairobi. However, most sales were handled by the Mombasa ivory room where local agents for buyers in Europe and Asia were invited to twice-yearly auctions sponsored by the government (the last auction was held in 1976). The wildlife trophies came from animals shot by the game department, from animals found dead in parks and reserves and from the hauls of poachers who had been caught. A tiny fraction of the total originated from animals shot on private land (landowners were allowed to shoot animals that threatened their crops but had to surrender all trophies from them to the game department—since colonial days all wildlife has belonged to the state). For convenience, the Ugandan parks and game department also sold their wildlife products at the Kenyan auctions.

Ivory was always the most valuable of the trophies at auction, and the two governments earned considerable revenue from its sale. With an eye to the international market, Kenya and Uganda together published catalogues on forthcoming auctions, listing the amount and quality of items available. Mombasa became renowned for the regularity, the quantity and quality of its ivory sales. Many of the buyers bid for rhino horn as well which they passed on to the pharmaceutical trade at a considerable profit. Other wildlife trophies sold in the Mombasa ivory room were hippo teeth; leopard, lion, cheetah, antelope, hyrax and crocodile skins; elephant and rhino feet and hides; and ostrich eggs. The ivory was classified into eight different categories, depending on size, weight, sex of the elephant and texture. But rhino horn was divided only into three kinds of lots, called "sound", "defective" or "rotten". In 1969 best quality ivory sold for six dollars a kilo and rhino horn for $32 a kilo. By 1978 the world market price was $65 a kilo for wholesale ivory, $300 a kilo for rhino horn.

The main factor in the sky-rocketing price of horn was, of course, increased demand from North Yemen; but there was another factor at work. In the 1970s new agents and buyers, many of whom were Africans, entered the trophies market in Kenya for the first time, broke the monopoly of the Gujarati dealers and introduced real competition into the proceedings. When the Africans began forcing up the prices, the Indians had to bid more just to stay in business. At the same time officialdom began to play a role in the auctions: nationalistic policies worked against the Indians, and those with direct access to licensing authorities found that there were means of displacing the former monopolists in the ivory and rhino trade.

Once the prices began to soar in East Africa, it was up to the buyers in Singapore, Macao, Hong Kong, Japan, Taiwan and South Korea (and later North Yemen) to raise their own offers—and this they willingly did in the mid 1970s, since these countries were all at this time experiencing tremendous economic growth.

Unfortunately for East Africa's rhinos, the price of horn started to rise just when the morale of the staff in the parks and reserves had fallen to a very low ebb. This coincidence was a boon for the poachers. In the 1970s, also, resourceful middlemen in Nairobi discovered that it was quite easy to fly rhino horn labelled "personal effects" out of the country on commercial airlines to such destinations as Hong Kong and Antwerp. Later, journalists began exposing the smuggling scandals after the Kenya government had officially banned all trade in wildlife and the airlines became much more cautious. Consequently, by the late 1970s most of the rhino horn illicitly moved out of Kenya went on steamships and dhows. Some called in at Somali ports where the rhino horn was transshipped to North Yemen. A staggering 40 per cent of all the rhino horn coming onto the world market between 1972 and 1978 ended up in North Yemen.

Still in 1980 Tanzania held legal sales of rhino horn. A parastatal organization, the Tanzania Wildlife Corporation (Tawico for short), acting on behalf of the government, was selling rhino horn to foreign buyers for hard cash. The previous year buyers from Kenya and North Yemen were paying Tawico between $280 and $300 a kilo for rhino horn. That which did not go directly to North Yemen was mostly re-sold by the buyers to Antwerp for export to Asia.

In Tanzania it is also possible for local dealers to buy rhino horn legally from the game department. In 1979 the price in Tanzanian shillings was equivalent to between $268 and $304 a kilo. Four or five of these local dealers had permits to export horn and their price to overseas buyers was between $400 and $500 a kilo.

Although in 1979 the Tanzanian government ratified CITES, which prohibits member states from importing or exporting rhino horn, at least one foreign buyer purchased rhino horn from Tawico in 1980. Kes Hillman, Chairman of IUCN African Rhino Group, also confirmed, following her trip to Dar es Salaam in July 1980, that local dealers were continuing to trade in rhino horn.

Farther south, in Zimbabwe, the government auctioned 159 kilos of rhino horn between 1959 and 1965. This horn was obtained from animals legitimately shot and from confiscated poachers' caches. The main buyers were local traders and representatives from South African export firms. How much additional rhino horn from Zimbabwe reached international markets is unknown, but in the late 1960s poaching was a severe problem. If the rhino censuses are to be believed, some 300 rhinos disappeared then. One of the hardest hit areas was the Chizarira National Park where Batonga tribesmen, using steel cables stolen from mining and drilling operations, snared 60 rhinos between 1965 and 1968. The government conducted a translocation programme between 1965 and 1975, which involved moving rhinos into the better protected parks and private wildlife estates. The programme seems to have been successful since rhino numbers have increased in recent years.

According to Dr Dave Cumming, Chief Ecologist of the Zimbabwe Department of National Parks, the government held only three rhino horn auctions in the 1970s, two in 1978 and one on 29 March 1979. The horns for these auctions came from the confiscated hauls of poachers, from animals found snared, losses in translocation, and from rhinos that had died naturally. In the two auctions held in Salisbury in 1978, there were 57 horns of which 24 came from the Middle Zambezi Valley, 24 from Wankie National Park and nine from other areas. The total weight of these horns was only 78.65 kilos, and the selling price was around $195 a kilo. South African dealers were the main buyers at the 1978 auctions; and in 1979, all the horn went to one dealer from Pretoria: 49 kilos at a price of just $186 a kilo. Since 1980 no horn has been sold from the parks; in fact, when I was in Salisbury in August 1981, the Department of Parks showed me 150 kilos that they were simply storing in a safe, with the intention of keeping the horn there indefinitely.

Johannesburg in the 1970s became the main trading centre for wildlife products in southern Africa, handling trophies from a catchment area including Angola, Mozambique, Botswana, South West Africa, Zambia and Zaire. Many of these surrounding countries were politically and economically unstable; residents who were in positions to obtain wildlife products sent them to South Africa in order to obtain cash which they could invest outside the spheres of their own governments. There was even a period in 1975 and 1976 during which thousands of Portuguese and Africans fled from the civil war that was raging in Angola and crossed the border to South West Africa with massive amounts of wildlife products to sell for whatever price they could get. When I was in South West Africa in November 1981, a mining prospector told me that in 1975 one of these refugees had approached him with a pair of rhino horns for which he was asking $180, a fair market price at the time. The prospector said he was not interested; however, the seller kept lowering his price, which finally dropped to $37 for the pair. Still protesting that he was not interested, the prospector drove off. When he returned home he discovered that the Angolan had given up trying to sell his horns and had simply dumped them into the back of the prospector's pick-up.

Conditions continued to deteriorate in Angola, and in the latter part of the decade some people survived by poaching whatever they could and selling rhino horn and ivory to South West Africa. The South West government indirectly encouraged the poachers by issuing to buyers proper documents so that the ivory and rhino horn could be legally imported into other countries. Traders from Johannesburg told me that they regularly went up to Rundu, on the border between South West Africa and Angola, during the 1970s to buy wildlife products. On occasion, some Portuguese would arrange business meetings with the traders to find out what they especially wanted, then they would return to Angola to procure the goods. This, in fact, was how the trade in rhino hide began between South Africa and South-East Asia. The Johannesburg dealers made enquiries in Hong Kong to find out if there were any rhino products other than horn in demand and learnt that there was a major market for rhino hide. Then they told their Portuguese contacts to bring in pieces the size of a square metre, which were sun-dried and not salted—specifications from Hong Kong. One Johannesburg trader said that from 1976 until 1979 he purchased about 1,000 kilos of dried hide and 600 kilos of horn, which he estimated was probably around 40 per cent of what was being marketed in Rundu then. Just before the major Portuguese exodus in 1975 there were between 500 and 1,000 rhinos in southern Angola, according to Brian Huntley, who had been employed by the Angolan government as an ecologist for the national parks. But, from 1975 onwards, the Portuguese and

Kes Hillman, of the IUCN African Rhino Group, and Esmond Bradley Martin measure rhino horns collected by officials of the Pilanesberg Game Reserve, Bophuthatswana.

Africans shot many of the rhinos in the Cuando Cubango area and even some of the 30 remaining in the Iona National Park.

It was not until 1979, when the authorities in South West Africa closed the border to Angola as a result of attacks from SWAPO guerrillas, that rhino products and ivory stopped changing hands in Rundu. Since then, Angolan rhino horn (what little is still available) has gone mainly into Botswana for re-export to Japan and Singapore. As a member of the South African Customs Union, Botswana can send whatever goods it wants to export via Jan Smuts International Airport in Johannesburg. The South African government, even though it has ratified CITES, does not intercept any wildlife shipments from members of the Customs Union that pass through its own borders. Moreover, the South African government does not enforce CITES regulations in any of the so-called independent homelands. Thus there are still consignments of rhino horn passing out of Jan Smuts which end up being called "South African exports" in the statistics of importing countries. For political reasons, the South African government has done nothing to close this loophole for rhino horn exports. Consequently, poaching for the international trade still goes on.

South West Africa is a case in point. While the estimated 275 rhinos in Etosha National Park are very secure, those that exist outside, in Kaokoland and Damaraland, are not. They are the 'desert rhinos' and are unique in that they survive in climatic conditions that are quite extraordinary for any black rhinos. In 1975 when P.J. ("Slang") Viljoen began to study the desert rhinos, there were 20 in Kaokoland and 80 in Damaraland. Now there are only seven in Kaokoland (three adult males and four adult females) and 50 in Damaraland. Although the rhinos must compete for the vegetation and water to some extent with domestic stock belonging to nomads, which accounts for some losses, poaching is their main threat. In 1981 a minimum of six rhinos were shot solely for their horns. One had its horns removed by an electric chain saw which strongly suggests that a European, not an African, was responsible.

To lose any desert rhino is, to my mind, an irreparable tragedy. There is so little known about how these animals cope in this rugged region of 4,000,000 hectares, consisting of mountains up to 2,600 metres, sand dunes and gravel plains, that every possible effort should be made to preserve them. Very, very few foreigners have ever had the opportunity to see these rhinos; yet, watching them in desolate valleys in the afternoon, or flying over them when they are on mountain tops in the early morning, is one of the most spectacular experiences a naturalist can have. There is extremely little vegetation aside from that which sprouts from dry river beds; Kaokoland has had hardly any rain in the last six years. About 350 different plants exist in this huge region, and the rhinos eat almost all of them, including *Euphorbia damarana* which is poisonous to man and most other wildlife. On account of the scarcity of vegetation, the rhinos have to move long distances to feed; they have the largest home ranges of any population of black rhinos in Africa: up to 2,000 square kilometres. One rhino which Viljoen tracked for four days travelled 150 kilometres in search of food.

According to the official South African export figures, 149.5 kilos of rhino horn went to Asia in 1978, excluding about fourteen trophy horns sent out of the country to France, West Germany, Spain and Taiwan, which came from animals legally shot by hunters. The 149.5 kilos represent horn collected and sold by the Natal Parks Board. However, this figure fails to tally with Hong Kong's statistics for imports of rhino horn from South Africa: six consignments, between June 1978 and February 1979, weighing a total of 344.7 kilos. Also, Japan recorded imports of 350 kilos of horn from South Africa in 1978, and Taiwan 166 kilos. In 1978 the Natal Parks Board stopped selling rhino horn in order to comply with CITES regulations; by November 1981 the Board had on hand 101 horns which were locked up in a safe at headquarters in Pietermaritzburg. The Natal Parks Board was the main source of rhino horn in South Africa; the amount of horn available from other parts of the country was very small indeed. Furthermore, by late 1979 the authorities in the Transvaal, the Orange Free State and the Cape Province had all prohibited the export of rhino products, except for sportsmen's trophies. However, in 1980 Japan's official statistics recorded 587 kilos of rhino horn from South Africa. What happened was that horn originating in Angola, Zambia, South West Africa and Tanzania was being supplied via South Africa.

The Natal Parks Board and the other government wildlife departments in South Africa have not had any real idea of the value of rhino horn. Instead of holding open auctions with bidders from the major importing countries, the Natal Parks Board simply invited tenders from traders they knew. In 1966 the Natal Parks Board sold 604 kilos of rhino horn to the Manica Cycle Company in Salisbury for $11.50 a kilo, but in that same year the average price in the Mombasa auction rooms was around $24 a kilo. Again in 1978 the Natal Parks Board sold rhino horn, for which they received the ridiculously low figure of $37 from a trader in Pretoria. The major importing countries (Japan, South Korea and Hong Kong) were then paying around $300 a kilo. Obviously, no one on the Natal Parks Board thought of contacting traders in Asia to request an estimate of the true value of African rhino horn.

In the 1970s countries in Asia received most of their rhino hide from South Africa. Aside from that which Johannesburg traders bought at Rundu, there was also some available from private ranches in Natal. I know that one trader bought between 400 and 500 kilos of dried hide from one source in Natal in 1978 and 1979 for only $17.50 a kilo. Yet another trader used to take a truck from Pretoria to Natal to go around the various ranches and buy up raw hide; in 1979 he paid about $28 a kilo for it. Since rhino hide at that time was selling retail for $427 a kilo in Hong Kong, Macao and Taipei, the ranchers were losing quite a bit of the profit.

There are two main reasons why South Africa has supplied most of the rhino hide to the Asian market. First, the wildlife traders in other African countries are unaware of its value. Secondly (and this would still apply even if the price were known), it is too risky for poachers to bother with. Soon after being removed from the animal it must be dried, and this involves poachers staying near the kill site for several days—which they obviously avoid doing. Even when dried, rhino hide is cumbersome and awkward to carry through the bush, and practically impossible to conceal in any quantity.

Among the rhino horn consumer nations, North Yemen is unique: it imports three times more horn than any other country and yet has no pharmaceutical use for it; furthermore, very few Yemenis are involved in orchestrating the horn imports. Those Yemenis who do participate in the trade, however, have proved willing to pay the highest prices in the world for African rhino horn. They began buying in a conspicuous manner at the Mombasa ivory auctions in 1975 and 1976, the last two years that these were held. One Arab from North Yemen bought 655 kilos in 1975 at an average price of $76 per kilo—more than double the world market price at the time. After the Mombasa auctions were stopped, most of the legitimate purchases made by the few Yemenis handling horn imports were from Tawico and private Tanzanian dealers. They also obtained some horn from Antwerp, which became Europe's major entrepot for rhino horn in the 1970s—a time when the supply of ivory from East and central Africa increased notably as a result of poaching.

Since there is no restriction on rhino horn imports into North Yemen, the

A rhino's "horn" is not in fact a true horn but made up from millions of tightly compacted hair-like fibres.

buyers have no need to document the legitimacy of their sources; and, because the demand is so great in North Yemen, they buy horn wherever they can. Agents in East Africa smuggle horn out for Yemeni buyers, using whatever transport is available. Somali tribesmen are quite willing, for a price, to carry poached Kenyan rhino horn on the backs of their donkeys and camels across the border into Somalia where it is transferred onto dhows for shipment to the Yemeni coast around Mocha. From there, lorries transport the rhino horn to the capital city. Other shipments come more directly by air.

One main wholesaler supplies rhino horn to the *djambia* handle-makers in the Sanaa souk. In late 1978 he was selling horn to them for $677 a kilo. The chain of profit-taking is long: after the carvers have made their handles, the shavings are collected from the souk. In 1978 shavings were being sold on the Hong Kong market for $150 a kilo. In 1979, after Hong Kong banned the import of rhino products, horn shavings from North Yemen were selling for $300 a kilo on the Chinese mainland.

Between 1949 and 1971, only 13 kilos of rhino horn were officially exported from East Africa to India. As usual, the statistics only tell part of the story. In fact, quite large consignments of rhino horn came into India during this period. One of the major ivory importers in India told me that when Kenya, Tanzania and Uganda became independent, many Indian residents decided to leave and took ivory and rhino horn with them for sale to traders in Bombay and in the state of Gujarat. In the 1970s, however, the smuggling of East African rhino horn to supply the Indian domestic market practically ceased. Rhino horn imports and exports were made illegal in India in 1972, in an attempt to cut down on the poaching of Indian rhinos. Whilst Indians have their ways of circumventing customs, the selling price for African rhino horn in India is too low to warrant the effort of smuggling very much into the country.

When I studied the traditional medicine shops in Bombay, Baroda, Ahmedabad and Delhi on my 1980 visit to India, I found very little rhino horn or skin on sale. The shopkeepers spoke openly with me. Not so long ago, they said, they did buy rhino horn which must have been smuggled into the country; in recent years, however, little had been offered to them by traders. They told me that they were able to prescribe substitutes to serve the same purposes as rhino horn. In general, their clients did not seem to be bothered by the fact that there was little rhino horn on the market—probably they had just as much faith in other products.

Even in northern parts of India and West Bengal, where Indian rhino horn is available, there is little to be found in the traditional medicine shops. In the past, however, there was a strong demand for it, and the story is told of a certain Major Cock who, in the late nineteenth century, saw some African horns in Calcutta which were much cheaper than Indian horns on sale in Assam. Knowing that Assamese paid quite high sums for bits and pieces of Indian horn, he thought he would be able to make a small fortune from the African horns, some of which were more than three feet long. He bought all of them and had them transported to Assam. To his utmost disappointment the Assamese would not purchase a single one because they did not believe they were genuine. Some time later, Major Pollok saw the horns Cock had purchased lying about on the floor of a teahouse in Gauhati, completely abandoned.

Because of the astronomically high prices that Indian rhino horn commands in the Chinese pharmaceutical trade, there is a great temptation for buyers in India to export it. No one can take rhino horn out of India legally; but, to take just one example, the Nepalese buyer from Kathmandu who bought most of the horn sold by the Assamese Forest Department in the 1970s would not have been able to dispose of it without loss for domestic use in India. In fact, I do not believe that the horn remained in India. When Indian traders buy rhino horn from the Assamese

Forest Department they are given official receipts and transit passes which permit them to transport the horn to other states within India. Occasionally, the authorities will later check to see what has happened to legally purchased rhino horn. If the buyer no longer has the horn, he may claim that his family made use of it for medicinal purposes—or he may produce a fake receipt showing that he sold it to another trader in a far-away part of India.

In an earlier chapter I mentioned the operation of poaching syndicates in India. Far more intricate are the smuggling syndicates, based in the large cities like Bombay, Delhi and Calcutta which have international airports and/or large seaports. Calcutta is the headquarters for many of the syndicates specializing in smuggling out wildlife products. This is because it is quite close to the huge forests of Assam and other places in north-east India where wildlife is still plentiful. Another advantage of Calcutta is its proximity to Bangladesh and Burma.

Wildlife preservation officers claim that the wildlife smuggling syndicates in Calcutta are headed by Gujaratis and Sindhis, not indigenous Bengalis. The Gujaratis are in fact the country's most notorious smugglers and do not confine their activities just to moving out wildlife products. A senior government officer employed to combat smuggling in Bombay told me that most of the illegal movement of silver out of India was organized by a Muslim Gujarati living in Damao, a former Portuguese colony on the west coast of India. This man, despite being known by name among the law enforcement agencies, has been able to avoid conviction because he has such a successful network of underlings to do his work that no proof can be established against him.

As well as rhino horn, syndicates export reptile and tiger skins. In 1979 some $625,000 worth of snake skins, destined for West Germany, were intercepted by government authorities in Calcutta. The syndicates use many different ploys to get wildlife products out of India. Sometimes they persuade airline crews, on 24-hour stop-overs, to carry contraband in their luggage when they leave. Diplomats are not immune to the pressures of smuggling syndicates, either. When all else fails, contact can be made with dhowmen in and around Bombay who will take wildlife products to Dubai for re-export to consumer countries.

As far as I am aware, and I did talk to several senior officers concerned with smuggling, the Indian government has been unable to prosecute a single rhino horn smuggler in recent years. In 1978 a small package of rhino horn was discovered by the authorities on its way to Japan. The package bore a return address and hopes were raised that at last it might be possible to crack one of the links in a smuggling syndicate. No such luck; the address turned out to be that of one of Calcutta's large cemeteries.

Unlike many countries in the Third World, India has made a sincere effort to stop the smuggling of wildlife products. However, with such big profits to be made, and with such well co-ordinated syndicates controlling the trade, there is only so much that the authorities can do. In 1972 the government passed the Wildlife (Protection) Act which prohibited, except under very extraordinary conditions, export of all rhino products. Soon afterwards, a number of wildlife preservation officers were appointed. They now serve under the Ministry of Agriculture and Irrigation and are posted in the main cities of Bombay, Delhi, Calcutta and Madras—the only centres from which any wildlife products can now be legally exported. Co-operating with customs officials and local state authorities, the wildlife preservation officers do what they can; however, Indian rhino horns are small—usually under three-quarters of a kilo—and can easily be camouflaged.

The Indian government ratified the CITES regulations in 1976, and in 1979 passed a law stating that "every consignment of wildlife and its products will be subject to verification by the Regional Director of Wildlife Preservation". But rules and regulations are useless without enforcement. Smuggling is a livelihood for thousands and thousands of Indians, and the illegal movement of wildlife products is just a small worry for the authorities relative to other priorities. Corruption is also a problem—perhaps inevitably since the smuggling business is worth hundreds of millions of dollars a year. Prosecution of dishonest businessmen is also difficult, since absolute proof is necessary to convince a judge and jury of an individual's guilt. India is not a police state, and for anyone to be convicted of an offence a proper trial must be held.

Ironically, the majority of Indian rhino horn available to smuggling syndicates is sold legally by the Assamese Forest Department. Illegal exports could be significantly decreased if the Forest Department stopped selling horn. From 1965 to 1975 Japanese traders imported 180 kilos of horn from India and from 1973 to 1977 South Korea imported 49 kilos from India, according to these countries' own official import statistics. I saw more Indian horn for sale in Taipei's pharmaceutical shops than anywhere else, but it was also widely available in smaller quantities in Singapore and Hong Kong. Because importers are willing to pay outrageous prices for Indian rhino horn, the syndicates are going to continue to smuggle it out of India in return for hard currency and a profit, no matter what obstacles the Indian government tries to set up.

The 1949 Communist Revolution in China had a profound impact on the British Crown Colony of Hong Kong, which until then had served mainly as an entrepot for goods passing to and from China. Strained relations reduced China's share in Hong Kong's trade to about a tenth by 1962. In order to survive Hong Kong had to industrialize quickly and develop a flair for innovation. The history of the ivory importers in the 1950s and 1960s well illustrates the ingenuity of the people of Hong Kong to turn what could have been a disaster into an economic boon.

Until World War II, Canton had been the main centre outside India for ivory carving. Since the early 1900s, Hong Kong importers had been supplying the factories there with considerable quantities of raw ivory. But communism and the commercial interests of the ivory carvers made strange bed-fellows. Prudently, many of the carvers from the Chinese mainland fled to Hong Kong, taking with them technical skills and a determination to prosper in the capitalist-orientated colony. The migration raised Hong Kong to pre-eminence in the world ivory trade. The carvers worked very hard and were paid not for their time but for the number of items they produced. Hong Kong consequently became the world's greatest ivory importer by 1958, surpassing even India, and the traders became involved in every aspect of the ivory business, expanding into exports of carved ivory jewellery, figurines and an amazing variety of curios, as well as opening up retail shops in Hong Kong for the sale of these items to the floods of tourists in search of bargains.

I had the opportunity to visit some of the ivory factories and watched Cantonese craftsmen turn out traditional and modern types of carvings with lightning speed. Many of them have discarded their old hand tools in favour of dentists' drills, and, as they work, clouds of ivory dust fill the air. Some of the ivory carvers work at home, rather than in factories, and I went to see one old man in a dingy apartment building, several flights up a dark staircase. He was surrounded by children and grandchildren who had learnt the art from him and, because of their productivity, the family income was over $25,000 a year. There are about 2,200 ivory carvers in Hong Kong now, and they each earn an average of $420 a month (carvers on the mainland make $50 a month). The wholesale price of an ivory carving in Hong Kong reflects the higher cost of labour there, although the quality is rarely as good as that of pieces carved on the mainland. Mainland carvers—there are around 7,000 left—spend much more time on each piece they make and, because they rarely use electric tools, they achieve a much finer finish on their work. Also, despite their greater numbers, they use less raw ivory than their cousins in Hong Kong—40 to 60 tons a year as against 200 to 300 tons.

In 1978 there were 52 major ivory-importing businesses in Hong Kong; of these, between 12 and 15 also handled imports of rhino products. As mentioned in an earlier chapter, rhino horn and ivory imports often go hand in hand because they have the same sources. In fact, from 1949 until North Yemen's new-found affluence in the mid 1970s, Hong Kong imported more rhino horn than any other country. Despite this experience, Hong Kong importers seem to know little about the use of rhino products. They have not involved themselves in any processing of rhino horn or hide for medicinal purposes; instead they have sold direct to pharmaceutical firms or re-exported to mainland China, Macao, Taiwan, Singapore, Japan, South Korea, Malaysia and Indonesia.

As an important group of businessmen, the ivory traders formed the Hong Kong and Kowloon Ivory Manufacturers Association in 1966 to protect their interests. They have since held monthly meetings, gathering for meals at the big hotels to discuss mutual problems and developments in various aspects of the ivory business. Occasionally, the subject of rhino horn comes up in these meetings, and a few years ago one importer related an incident that cost him dearly. He had been offered rhino horn shavings from South Yemen which he bought sight-unseen and had shipped by air to Hong Kong at his own expense, knowing that there was an agent from the Chinese mainland interested in the purchase. But when he tried to re-sell the shavings to the agent, it was discovered that the ivory importer had been tricked: the gunny bags held cow horn shavings instead.

Among other problems that Hong Kong's ivory association deals with are those that have arisen from conservationists' appeals. Especially since the 1960s wildlife conservation organizations throughout the world have grown in popularity and public support. Well aware of the power that the conservationists wield as a result of their various campaigns to try to protect endangered species, the ivory traders in Hong Kong have kept a wary eye on their activities. They do not wish to come into conflict with them, for to do so could cost them a lot of money. They did not oppose the Hong Kong government's introduction of the Animals and Plants Ordinance in 1976 which was supposed to conform with the CITES convention. However, they must have had a good laugh when they realized that the ordinance still permitted import/export of rhino products, albeit with licences, even though this was expressly forbidden by CITES. What was even more ludicrous was that the people responsible for drafting Hong Kong's law used the term "rhinoceros species" which technically refers only to Javan and Indian rhinos, so products of the other three rhinos could still come in and leave Hong Kong legally without any licensing whatsoever. The law stood for two years before "rhinoceros species" was changed to cover all rhinos. Afterwards, the Director of Agriculture and Fisheries became responsible for issuing the licences for any rhino products, and he did so when he was convinced that they were legally exported from their countries of origin, e.g. Zambia, Tanzania and South Africa.

At the end of 1978 when Ian Parker was carrying out a major survey of the international ivory trade for the US Fish and Wildlife Service, he discussed the rhino poaching problem in East Africa with ivory importers in Hong Kong. He advised the dealers to cease all trade in rhino commodities. They agreed and took the initiative of approaching the Director of Agriculture and Fisheries to request him not to issue any further import or export licences for new rhino products; since 23 February 1979 not one has been granted.

Later in 1979 when I was doing research in South-East Asia on rhino products, it was obvious to me that Hong Kong's ban on imports and exports of rhino products had been strictly adhered to. Since the dealers themselves initiated this action, I believe it will continue to be successful.

Less than an hour away from Hong Kong by jetfoil across the South China Sea lies the Portuguese colony of Macao. In the sixteenth century it was a very important and prosperous port of call for Portuguese ships plying between the Indies and Japan, but when the Dutch usurped the Eastern trade a hundred years later Macao fell into decline; it has only been during the last decade that its economy has begun to revive.

In the 1960s the basis of Macao's economy was its free exchange market and the sale of gold. Industrialization was limited to mass-production of match-boxes and fire-crackers. In those years mainland China put extreme pressure on Macao and demanded impossible concessions from the staid Portuguese governor. However, the communists soon enough decided that, in the long run, Macao was worth more to them as a window to the Western world than as an integral part of China. So by the 1970s the citizens of Macao had settled down with relative security to the serious pursuit of commercialization. By the second half of that decade new textile factories had helped to double the value of exports, and tourism was growing by leaps and bounds.

Most of Macao's visitors are Chinese from Hong Kong who turn up on week-ends and public holidays for the purpose of gambling. New casinos dominate the sky-line; one looks like a giant pot of marmalade. Day and night roulette, baccarat, craps, blackjack and one-armed bandits (called "Hungry Tigers" here) gobble up the hard-earned money of Hong Kong merchants, occasionally recompensing the lucky with a windfall, but absorbing thousands of dollars hourly for the coffers of the state.

This tiny territory has one of the highest population densities in the world: 300,000 people crammed into less than 16 square kilometres. Of these, 97 per cent are ethnic Chinese; the rest are Eurasian and Portuguese. The vast majority of Macaons are conservative in outlook, and many make use of the traditional Chinese medicine shops located in and around the Rua das Mercadores. I found that eight out of ten of Macao's traditional medicine shops sold rhino products, with the greatest demand being for processed rhino skin. Although pharmacists do not claim that skin has all the curative properties of rhino horn, it is a cheaper substitute in most cases. Moreover, whilst raw rhino hide in Hong Kong is scarce, it is plentifully available in Macao. In general, rhino products seemed to be less expensive in Macao than in Hong Kong—understandably, since the cost of living is much less in Macao and the overheads of shopkeepers are minimal.

Until Hong Kong banned international trade in rhino products, the owners of the medicine shops in Macao bought their supplies from the Hong Kong importers. The Department of Agriculture and Fisheries in Hong Kong asked me to try to discover if Macaons were now buying directly from Africa; however I could find no evidence of that at all. Instead, the pharmacists told me that they went to the Canton Trade Fairs at the invitation of the Chinese communists who offered them good discounts on the products they wanted to purchase as a good-will gesture. They were pleased with this development and said they intended to continue buying horn and skin from Canton for their businesses; since their contacts with other consumer countries were limited, they only purchased what they needed for themselves and did not re-export any rhino products.

I have not visited China, and even if I were able to go there, I doubt if the authorities would grant me the opportunity to collect the sort of information I would like to have on the trade and uses of rhino products today. Nevertheless, I do know from fieldwork elsewhere that mainland China has far-reaching influence on the use of animal-based drugs throughout Asia and that it is also the major exporter of tablets purported to contain rhino horn.

Traditional medicine in China went into a decline at the end of the nineteenth century. This was largely due to the efforts of foreigners like Benjamin Hobson who, after receiving his MD in London, went to Canton as a resident medical missionary, learnt Chinese and "deplored the sorry state of Chinese medicine". Later in Shanghai, between 1851 and 1858, he wrote and published in Chinese four text books intended to introduce local physicians to Western medical practice. The popularity of these books led to a proliferation of editions (one set was recently offered for sale by an antiquarian book dealer in New York for $1,800).

Under Chairman Mao, Chinese traditional medicine regained its former prestige. Not only did he decree that Western-type medical practice should be integrated with the traditional systems but he also set up special institutes for research into old Chinese theory. Dr Norman Miller, Professor of Community Medicine at Dartmouth Medical School, spent a month in 1979 in Peking, Shanghai and Sian studying Chinese medicine, and he reports that the new institutes are very active. Professor Ho Peng-Yoke has written that people all over China have recently been encouraged by the government to reveal their families' secret prescriptions for various afflictions. The two million "bare-foot doctors" in China in 1977 were trained in the rudiments of both traditional and Western medicine. One consequence of the resurgence of traditional practice has been a significant increase in demand for rhino horn in China. The Chinese imported 4,554 kilos in 1972 from Kenya alone and 2,225 kilos in 1973. In the past few years the Chinese have also been the major consumers of rhino horn shavings from North Yemen. I believe that the Chinese use the shavings mainly in the manufacture of low-cost drugs, both for export and domestic use, to treat many common ailments. One reason why these drugs are cheap is that the actual amount of rhino horn in them is very small indeed; other components such as herbs are used in much higher ratios.

Taiwan is a country which has a very great demand for rhino-based medicines—although, obviously, it does not import any preparations from China. Until 1979 the Taiwanese bought most of their rhino products from Hong Kong, and between 1972 and 1978 their imports averaged 943 kilos a year. Although they have also bought rhino horn and skin from South Africa, they have never purchased any directly from East Africa. The Taiwanese consume Indian rhino horn as well, and one sees both types for sale in the same shop. The pharmacists are worried about how they will be able to replenish their Indian horn supplies now, since all of it used to come in through dealings with Hong Kong traders. This concern is evident in the exorbitant retail price of Indian horn: $17,000 on average for a kilo, whilst African horn sells for $1,600 a kilo. Of course, no patient would require anything like a kilo of horn; a prescription consists of one to three grams.

The importers and wholesalers of rhino products in Taiwan are centred in Taipei, mostly in Di Hwa Street, but there are several small lanes leading off it which are also lined with wholesale shops selling rhino horn, skin and other traditional pharmaceuticals. These shops are unattractive, dingy, noisy and polluted—very different from the elegant retail pharmacies in Taipei. Gunny bags, barrels, boxes and other containers of various items clutter the floor space, and one has to climb over them in some shops in order to approach the sales counter. When electric machines are in use, grinding roots and twigs for packaged medicinal preparations, the dust which is produced clogs one's lungs; conversations are limited to shouting orders and replies over the din. Old and young men alike scurry around, producing herbs from here, an antler from there and heaping mounds of odd concoctions into bags for the demanding pharmacists. Usually there is a back room in these shops where the owner and his employees can take short breaks from their tedious work. But the noise is still ear-splitting there when a game of mah-jong is going on.

When I talked to the wholesalers I learnt that Taiwan does not restrict the imports of rhino products, although a 24 per cent import duty has to be paid on whatever is brought in. The wholesalers said they would probably buy more rhino horn from South Africa in the future because of the rarity of Indian horn. They also said that they presumed they would continue to be able to buy black rhino horn from other Asian entrepots, which I took to mean Singapore in particular. More than one dealer told me that many Taiwanese have in their homes pieces of rhino horn as keepsakes, and it was thought that with its high price now quite a bit of it will eventually come onto the local market. When I asked how much rhino horn was privately held, I was told there was at least a thousand kilos!

The Hong Kong ban has not been in effect long enough to tell what influence it will have on Singapore, but I would guess that this country will take over as Asia's main entrepot for rhino products. Singapore has very good trade links with other countries, excellent communications and shipping facilities. More to the point, Singapore has few restrictions on wildlife products and is in fact already notorious for dealing in endangered bird species. No conservation groups seem to be active locally, nor has the government shown any inclination towards signing CITES, apparently content to turn a blind eye to the large-scale animal traffic which has enriched many traders. A few wholesalers told me that they were supposed to obtain import licences for rhino horn now, but they usually did not bother to do so since they could claim on their customs forms that it was traditional medicine which could thereby enter the country freely.

I found rhino horn for sale not just in traditional medicine shops in Singapore, but also in ivory wholesale outlets (one proprietor said that he had bought 200 kilos of rhino horn from East Africa in 1977). The modern shopping complexes also stock rhino horn, and I even found some in the pharmacy shop of an international-class hotel. An apothecary on one of the most expensive shopping streets said that ten years ago rhino horn was cheaper in Singapore than deer antlers; others later confirmed this statement. My very highly educated guide in Singapore told me that every time he had a sore throat as a child his mother would treat it with rhino horn shavings steamed in water. He said he had drunk so much of it that he never wanted to see any again!

"... Thailand is one of the worst ecological disaster zones", wrote a reporter in *Asiaweek* (21 September 1979), and I do not think any conservationist would wish to contradict this statement. Thailand once boasted the richest variety of wildlife in all South-East Asia, with equatorial fauna in the southern jungles and temperate creatures in the northern provinces. Only relatively recently have people begun to realize the uniqueness of Thailand's wildlife heritage; scores of species have been discovered there this century; but many species have also become extinct in Thailand during the last 100 years. For instance, scientists first identified the kouprey, a large cow-like animal, in 1937. It was last reliably sighted in Thailand in 1948. However, there were reports of a herd migrating to the Dongrak mountains in 1976, which prompted two different groups of scientists to set off in search of them. They discovered past traces of the animals. They also found themselves surrounded by dozens of illegal hunters.

Lack of control over hunting is in fact the most inexcusable of the calamities that beset wildlife in Thailand. In 1973 a Royal Thai Army helicopter crashed near Bangkok. Investigations revealed that it had been used by some members of a large hunting party, including police and defence officials, who had gone shooting in the "protected" Thung Yai game reserve. The crash had resulted from the helicopter being overloaded with game carcasses.

Wanton slaughter of animals is, however, only partially accountable for the loss of so much of Thai wildlife. Another culprit is economic development. Whilst Thailand had a long history as the world's foremost producer and exporter of teak

On following pages. Left The veterinarian in charge repeatedly checks the respiration and heartbeat of the rhino during a translocation.

Right In order to transport a drugged rhino to its new home, the animal is tied onto a wooden sledge for loading onto a truck.

When tracking a rhino by helicopter, in order to dart it for translocation, the pilot tries to head the animal into a spacious, open area.

Aware that the helicopter overhead is tracking a rhino, the people in the area quickly flee in order to avoid a possible charge by the rhino.

An official of Kenya's Wildlife Conservation and Management Department loads a dart with the synthetic morphine drug, Immobilon, for use in capturing black rhinos.

Having arrived at a holding ground, a drugged rhino is pushed and pulled into an enclosure to recover from the effects of the anaesthetic.

Opposite In Kenya, a rhino is totally immobilized, strapped to a sledge, with cushions placed under its head before being transported. The more advanced technique, used in Natal today, is to keep the animal on its feet in a dazed condition in which it can be walked into a crate.

On following pages Most Kenyans today rarely see a rhino, so when this rhino was captured, word quickly spread and many people came to watch.

Recovering from the effects of the anaesthetic, and finding itself in completely foreign surroundings after capture, the black rhino is very dangerous. For the first couple of days it is likely to charge at the slightest noise or movement.

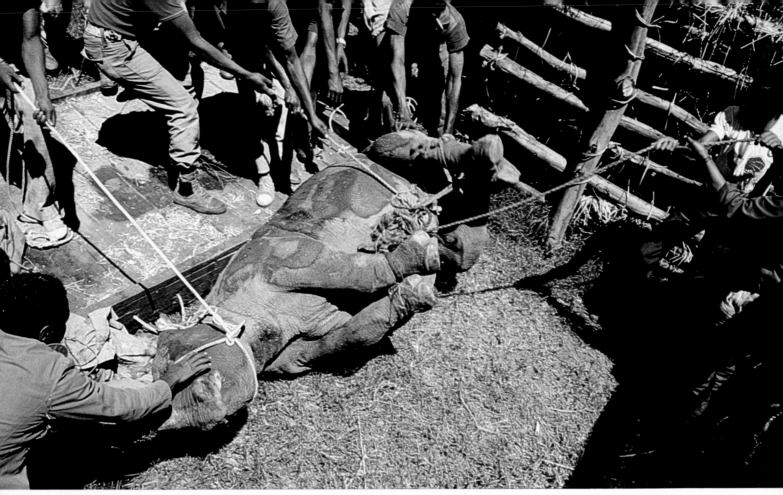

This black rhino, being pulled off a sledge into a stockade after capture, has two patches of open sores involving blood-sucking flies which are then often kept open by ox-pecker birds. Such skin lesions are commonly found on black rhinos.

After several days in a small enclosure, the black rhino becomes used to humans and welcomes its daily bath.

(in the late 1800s there were approximately 20,000 domesticated elephants working in the teakwood forests), it has only been during the last few decades that deforestation has reached epidemic proportions. In living memory, forests covered some 80 per cent of the country's land mass. By 1979, however, the forest cover was down to 25 per cent, in favour of logging, tin mining, rubber plantations and, of course, rice fields to feed the ever-growing human population.

It is the forests that have been the home of the most valued of Thai animals, including the clouded leopard and the Indochinese tiger. The forests were also the realm of the Javan rhinoceros (and a thousand horns were exported to China in just one year in the nineteenth century). No one knows for sure when the Javan rhino was finally wiped out in Thailand—it could have been as recently as the 1950s. Today it may even be too late to save the few remaining Sumatran rhinos in Thailand. Dr Boonsong Lekagul, who founded the first conservation society in this part of the world in 1947, doubts if there are even a dozen Sumatran rhinos left alive in Thailand today.

Dr Boonsong is an amazing character. An energetic 75-year-old medical doctor, he gave up hunting for sport after World War II, when he realized Thailand was "in danger of losing most of our wildlife treasures within my lifetime". He has waged battles with the authorities for the last thirty years to try to stop hunting and the trade in wildlife products in Thailand. A lot of his effort has been in vain. In 1961 the Wildlife Conservation Division of the Royal Forest Department was established to give protection to some of the endangered species; however, two of the nine most endangered species were already extinct by the time the law was passed. Moreover, it was not until 1972 that restrictions were first introduced on the trade and possession of wildlife products. Even today, once a tiger's head has been made into an ashtray it can be bought quite legally since it is no longer considered a wildlife trophy.

There is not supposed to be any trade in Sumatran or Javan rhino products in Thailand, but even a cursory examination of the Chinese traditional medicine shops will show that this law is not enforced. With so few Sumatran rhinos left in the country, new supplies of the horn are now coming from the Burmese frontier, north-west of Chiangmai and across the Tenasserim range west of Bangkok. Not all the Sumatran horn remains in Thailand; South Korean statistics show imports from Thailand of 81 kilos in 1974, 65 kilos in 1976, and 66 kilos in 1977. It is possible that some of this may be of the Indian species, simply transshipped to Bangkok; but I do not believe that African horn is involved in these exports.

Traders in wildlife products in Thailand are quick to exploit new demands. A sorry example of this is that when they realized the Thai people were becoming more interested in animals as pets in Bangkok in the 1960s, they began displaying for sale all kinds of creatures at the week-end Pramane market. In the early 1970s it was common to see gibbons, tapirs, pangolins, otters and many rare species of birds and reptiles being bought cheaply by Chinese and Thais and taken home cooped up in small cages to entertain their families. In the middle 1970s a few animal sympathizers, led by Dr Boonsong, began to complain vociferously to the authorities (Joy Adamson visited the market and was so shocked by what she saw that she donated a considerable sum of money "to publicize these horrors"). Some action was eventually taken against the pedlars of endangered species. When I visited the week-end market in September 1979, only the more common types of Thai wild animals were being offered for sale, such as monkeys ($100 each), mongooses (also $100), squirrels ($10), turtles (25¢), crickets (10¢) and various fighting fish and song birds. These creatures, however, were still being displayed in cages far too small for them, and the trade was brisk.

Thailand's conservation problems are acute, and the trade in rhino products is small relative to the whole. Some of the apathy towards law enforcement may be

The Sumatran is the most primitive of the five extant rhino species.

due, as conservationists claim, to unscrupulous dealers who succeed in corrupting officials by paying them bribes in order to exploit illegal wildlife products. The main wildlife exporters in Bangkok probably number no more than half a dozen, and they are mostly Thais of Chinese origin. They are rich and influential people. Some of them are said to have developed clever tricks to elude customs inspectors, such as slipping a few Sumatran rhino horns into a crate of poisonous snakes. A few dealers are also suspected of taking products from endangered species to Laos. There fake documents are obtained claiming that the products are of Laotian origin. They are then brought back to Bangkok "in transit" for overseas destinations, e.g. Belgium, Japan and Taiwan.

Occasionally, the Thai authorities respond to international pleas against their general lack of interest in wildlife. When I was in Bangkok there was a story going around about a restaurant advertising tiger penis soup to its clientele. Some officials of a worldwide conservation organization heard the story when they were passing through Bangkok. They went to the restaurant and verified that although the soup was not written on the menu, the waiters did offer it. The conservationists then went to the Wildlife Conservation Division and raised a storm. Shortly afterwards, the authorities raided the restaurant, confiscated three soggy male cat organs which were alleged to have been simmered in broth for a few minutes each time the brew was made, and arrested the owner of the restaurant.

Importers of rhino products in Asia generally obey the laws imposed and do not openly flout government regulations—so the Thais are somewhat atypical. The real problem with the trade is that the source countries do not appreciate the importance of conserving their wildlife. The importers—rightly or wrongly—contend that these countries "should put their own houses in order" to preserve stable wildlife populations and so meet the demands of the trade in an orderly fashion.

A member of the Teleki-von Hohnel expedition shoots rhinos in the vicinity of Lake Turkana in Kenya, an area where they are now extinct.

6 · Prospects for Rhinos

The world's rhino population fell by about 50 per cent between 1970 and 1979. If the decline is not to become irreversible, then ideally an immediate halt should be brought about to both poaching and the trade in rhino products. We all know that it is impossible to achieve these objectives in full; but some conservation measures can be implemented, and stricter controls on the trade are feasible. At this point in the rhino's plight, even half-way measures are desirable to help prolong the survival of some of the populations.

Two of the Asian species, the Javan and Sumatran, face the bleakest prospects simply because there are so few of them left. Both of these rhinos have been hard hit by human encroachment on their habitat; indeed, the only reason there are any Javan rhinos left is that they retreated to the dense jungles and swampy valleys of the very western tip of Java in the early part of the twentieth century. This is an inhospitable environment, unwanted for development projects, despite Indonesia's population increase of three million a year. Today, however, the Javan rhinos are no longer safe even there; about one-third of them fell victim to poachers in the early 1960s. Were it not for the basic aid schemes that the World Wildlife Fund has since laid on, it is possible that not a single Javan rhino would be alive today.

The history of WWF activity in the Udjung Kulon Nature Reserve, the last home of the Javan rhinos, shows how very basic these contributions have been. When Dr Lee Talbot went there in 1964 he recommended that a motor launch should be made available to facilitate the movement of supplies to those working in the reserve and for the use of those who in the future would carry out research on the animals. He also suggested that there should be a Land Rover to help in the patrolling of the area. Both the launch and the Land Rover arrived in 1967. Then, between November 1966 and March 1967 Dr Jacques Verschuren from Belgium attempted to carry out a preliminary survey of the rhinos. His work was seriously impeded by the west monsoon rains, but he reported that poaching seemed to be on the decrease and could be further controlled if the guard system were improved.

Drs Rudolf and Lotte Schenkel went to Udjung Kulon in April 1967 on WWF grants. During their seven-month stay, the number of guards was increased from ten to fourteen and, again thanks to WWF, improvements were made to the guards' huts, and each man received a new uniform, two pairs of shoes, a hat and a belt as well as a subsidized salary and more food. The Schenkels treated the guards when they were sick, provided them with malaria prophylaxis, and wrote in their report that the health of the guards "visibly improved over this period, most probably due to better nutrition". By providing food, clothing and subsistence wages to the guards, WWF secured better protection for the rhino population which increased from 25 in 1967 to about 50 in 1979.

As Chairman of the IUCN Survival Service Commission's Asian Rhino Group Dr Rudolf Schenkel has expressed concern that the Javan rhinos in Udjung Kulon may be facing a serious food shortage, and that this in turn could cut down their numbers. A study carried out by Hartmann Amman between December 1978 and May 1979 showed that some of the rhinos were moving considerable distances in search of food every night. Consequently, Dr Schenkel is now urging translocation of a breeding nucleus to another area, which would also lessen all the other obvious risks inherent in confining the one population to a single site. Since the Indonesian government opposes the removal of any of these animals to another country, Dr Schenkel suggests that a survey should be made of Sumatra to try to find a suitable second home for them there. However, Dr Schenkel also notes in his August 1979 report that the government "plans to phase out WWF contributions for the field staff in Udjung Kulon". Were that to happen, the efforts of the last fifteen years to give protection to the rhinos could turn out to have been wasted. All the evidence suggests that when the guards are not adequately provisioned, they cannot properly patrol the reserve, and poachers are quick to take advantage of the situation.

The authorities have also expressed their intention to open up Udjung Kulon to tourism, with the rhinos as the main attraction. There are flaws in this proposal. First, animals of dense forest jungle are extremely difficult to view. Tourists like to go where animals are tame, plentiful and easy to see. On these grounds alone it is unlikely that the Javan rhinos would be a successful lure for tourists. Secondly, tourism as a *raison d'être* is a poor basis for conservation; tourism is the most fickle of all businesses, and the most vulnerable to international political events. Thirdly, there is the point made by Ian Parker in the book he wrote with Laws and Johnstone, that developed areas, i.e. those providing the greatest access to tourists, are the most easily poached of all, for development gives access to poachers as well as to viewers. Tourist development in the absence of stable government and the manpower, will and ability to enforce the law, has led to the rape of several African national parks. Parker's point that true wilderness, unpenetrated by tracks and roads, is on its own one of the best defences for jungle animals should be considered carefully by the Indonesian Directorate of Nature Conservation. The Directorate must also be made aware of the weight of its responsibility in having in its charge the last remaining Javan rhinos in the wild.

Professor E.M. Lang once watched a pair of Indian rhinos copulate continuously for 83 minutes.

The Sumatran rhino is probably the best climber of the species, negotiating steep slopes where elephants would never venture and leaving his tracks at altitudes of 2,000 metres. He moves quickly, even at a walk, and although he is small in comparison to other rhinos a man cannot keep up with him at this pace; furthermore, when the rhino is aware of his arch enemy's presence he evades him with all kinds of tricks. Theodore Hubback, a very keen naturalist, spent forty days in a remote part of a Malayan jungle in the late 1930s tracking one old male. He came close to the rhino on several occasions, hearing him three times, but he never caught sight of him. Hubback wrote up his experiences for the *Journal of the Bombay Natural History Society*, noting that this rhino's habits "were fairly regular until he became alarmed and then he was the cunningest thing in the jungle". Such elusiveness, and the ability to survive in the most impenetrable of hilly rain forests, have enabled the Sumatran rhino to persist in the mountainous parts of Burma, Malaysia and Sumatra, and possibly in Thailand, Laos and Cambodia, despite threats from poachers who dig pits in their paths or plant sharp stakes in the steepest of their trails. The determination of the poachers to bag their prey appears to exceed that of the zoologists in most of their attempts to try to figure out where viable population units still exist. Reliable statistics are only available for Endau Rompin in Malaysia and Gunung Leuser in northern Sumatra.

Endau Rompin harbours between 20 and 25 Sumatran rhinos, and the state of Johore has turned 500 square kilometres of this area into a wildlife sanctuary. Since the rhino range extends into the adjacent state of Pahang, efforts are being made to win the authorities' support there for an additional area of 400 square kilometres of rhino territory. This is extremely important because in 1977/8 on the Pahang side a wide strip of forest cutting across the core area of the rhinos was logged. Rhinos now avoid this part of their range, but what is even more ominous

The Javan rhino looks similar to the Indian rhino; it is only slightly smaller, but as a forest dweller it only browses whereas the Indian rhino both grazes and browses.

is that since then no traces of immature rhinos have been found. The disturbance caused by deforestation would be even more serious if human intrusion and settlement were permitted along the tracks made by the loggers. Fortunately, it is likely that both sides of Endau Rompin will develop into a national park, but provision must be made for the training of an anti-poaching force and for scientists to study the ecology of the rhinos in order to discover their requirements.

Evidence of the presence of Sumatran rhinos has been found in five widely separated areas of Sumatra but the Gunung Leuser complex of reserves is believed to have the most, with between 50 and 100 individuals left, rendering it the most important target for conservation. Elephants, tigers, orangutans and clouded leopards also reside in Gunung Leuser. All these animals are jeopardized by the operations of timber companies, agricultural exploitation and inadequate management.

Since there are so many conflicts between nature conservation and the demands for other land uses, it would make sense to capture some Sumatran rhinos and move them to well-protected reserves or even zoos. In the nineteenth century a number of Sumatran rhinos were born in captivity and there were even two in the Barnum and Bailey circus at one time. The last captive Sumatran rhino died in the Copenhagen zoo in 1972. If a breeding stock could be established in a safe environment, perhaps some of the progeny could one day be returned to a preserved natural habitat in South-East Asia without fear of poachers.

Adequate management for conservation policies in Third World countries is indeed possible; a good example is that of the Indian rhino in Nepal and India. In providing protection for rhinos in major parks, these two governments are fulfilling a moral obligation to preserve a part of their wildlife heritage, and in so doing they have prevented the Indian rhino from becoming an endangered species. Inside Chitawan National Park is the world-famous Tiger Tops, a rustic game lodge attracting high-income tourists from all over the world, who pay $240 per couple a night to stay there to observe some of the 350 rhinos and other wild animals. Less well-heeled tourists stay at a nearby tented camp for $150 per couple. Visitors are welcome to climb onto the back of an elephant to wander about the park at a very leisurely pace, to take photographs, or simply revel at the sight of the animals in a natural setting of unsurpassed beauty. For those who wish to move around more quickly, or who do not have enough trust in a mount trained to stand its ground when face to face with a snorting rhino attempting a charge, there are Land Rovers also available. The Nepalese government earns much-needed hard currency from those foreigners who visit Chitawan, and its popularity is such that it has become the major tourist destination outside the Kathmandu valley, just a 35-minute flight from the capital to the Terai lowlands where the park is located.

In addition to the 950 rhinos in India's Kaziranga National Park there are 8,000 hog deer, 900 wild pigs, 800 elephants, 700 swamp deer, 660 water buffaloes and 100 barking deer. There are also tigers, leopards, sloth bears, otters, gaurs and monkeys. To my mind, Kaziranga is the finest wildlife reserve in all of Asia. Here transport by one of the park's 20 domesticated elephants is a must, for the swampy nature of the terrain limits the number of roads; however, setting out at dawn with a skilled mahout as your guide, with the snow-covered Himalayas gradually coming into view from the north and the lush plant life radiantly reflecting the early morning rays of the sun, is an unforgettable experience. Kaziranga's rhinos can be approached quite closely; they rarely start to grunt and push off until an elephant comes nearer than six metres, and they are unlikely to charge. In the event of a charge the elephant is ordered to stand still, for at the last moment the rhino will realize what it is up against and veer away. If the elephant does turn away from the charge it is quite likely that the rhino will give chase and try to nip it on the rump or tail.

Although Kaziranga welcomes visitors and accommodates them adequately and at a reasonable charge, the full tourist potential is far from being realized. One of the major drawbacks is the annual flooding of the Brahmaputra river which means that the park must be closed between May and late September. Another problem is that foreigners must obtain a special pass from the government to enter the state of Assam because it borders Bhutan, Bangladesh and Burma and is itself a region of political unrest. It is also difficult to reach Kaziranga. The nearest airport is 90 kilometres away at Jorhat—and getting to Jorhat involves first going to Calcutta, a city many foreigners prefer to avoid. Almost a million tourists go to India in a year, but only about one in a thousand of these currently visits Kaziranga.

The park could certainly use increased revenue from tourism for development purposes; but to give the Assam government its due, Kaziranga is already well managed. Even if, say, for political reasons, visitors could not come to Kaziranga, the authorities would continue to run the park efficiently and to provide protection for the rhinos. In fact, most areas in India set aside as reserves or wildlife sanctuaries are well protected, including those remote places which hardly any tourists visit. State authorities and the national government support the reserves, taking the business of conservation seriously, and they are fully backed by a powerful and influential lobby in India.

Rhinos in tropical Africa have only become seriously threatened in the past five or six years, and the main reason for their present predicament is the breakdown of law and order in many of the countries where their populations were once relatively stable. In the past, traditional hunting, hunting for sport and culling in order to clear the land depleted rhino numbers by thousands and thousands but did not endanger the species' prospects for survival. Quite early on, too, it was

This was the ninth baby born to an Indian rhino in the Basle zoo. It weighed 69 kilos.

realized that human population growth and economic development would sooner or later exert pressure on the land, with the result that most African countries that had tremendous numbers of various large wild mammals set aside parks and reserves for them. In such places as Botswana, Malawi, Zambia, Uganda, Tanzania and Kenya the game parks continued to flourish in the early years of independence; some countries even gazetted more areas for the sole purpose of wildlife preservation, finding that tourism was a prime foreign-exchange earner, and that the tourists were coming in greater and greater numbers mainly to see the wild animals. So, while many conservationists watched with sorrow the inevitable passing of the era when rhinos, elephants, leopards, lions and antelope roamed truly free on the African plains and in the forests, there was nevertheless comfort in the hope that many of these animals and others would remain relatively secure in the parks and reserves.

This hope, in many cases, was blighted. Lack of political stability in several African countries led to disregard for existing laws, inefficiency in the police and armed forces and severe failings in the judiciary systems—and in some instances civil war and revolution. Angola, Chad, the Central African Republic and Uganda have been amongst the worst hit. The Uganda lesson was a particularly hard one to learn, with convoys of food destined for starving Karamojong children being hijacked by armed bandits over whom no one exerted any control and who were equipped with vehicles and weapons secured through foreign aid. People do not like to believe that this sort of thing can happen, but it has, and there was certainly a time in 1979/80 when conservationists should have thought twice before donating money to organizations to spend more on vehicles, radios and other items for anti-poaching purposes in Uganda. Gifts like these are a waste of effort, time and scarce funds when there is no infrastructure left to provide protection for people, let alone wildlife. No one knows how much has been spent to establish Kabalega National Park in north-western Uganda, to support patrols and build up an administration for it. Whatever the amount, it did not keep the park from falling into the hands of gangs who, in 1979, 1980 and 1981, were using modern rifles on animals that could provide meat for the pot and trophies to be sold for cash. Park vehicles, provided by well-meaning animal sympathizers, were stolen, illegally sold, or simply wrecked.

Without the maintenance of security, respect for the law and an honest judiciary there is no hope of safe-guarding rhino populations. The very first step to be taken in any country before conservation action can be carried out with a chance of success is to ensure that law enforcement bodies are fully in control. And that is a matter for governments, not for outsiders. The fact is that many African countries no longer properly enforce the laws on their statute books pertaining to the illegal killing of wildlife. And poachers and middlemen, even when they are caught, tend to get off very lightly; they are often fined only a small percentage of the value of the trophies they have in hand. Time and time again this has happened in Kenya, Uganda, Tanzania and Zambia. The deterrent has become meaningless, so it is no wonder that the poachers are now active in these countries' parks and reserves.

The next most important step is to get top-quality personnel into the various government bodies dealing with game reserves and national parks. In several African countries the pay is so low, and the terms of service so unfavourable, that potential candidates do not even bother to apply for jobs in wildlife departments. The qualifications necessary for appointment are also often rather inappropriate: the man with a half dozen assorted diplomas is not usually the one with the greatest desire to live and work in remote areas. Formal education is just not as important, in the final analysis, as enthusiasm and dedication to wildlife. These qualifications cannot really be taught; but in training and hard work additional skills can be learnt—even road building and piloting an aircraft. Those who persevere in the lower echelons of service to parks and reserves should be encouraged with the possibility of obtaining higher status. Respect for heads of departments, especially in Africa, is hard won; but those who have risen to positions of responsibility through merit command a greater support from their subordinates and are more alert to the problems they face.

Of course, parks and reserves need four-wheel-drive vehicles, light aircraft and other modern equipment, but I feel that too much emphasis is placed on their use today. There is no substitute for the old-fashioned foot patrols combing game paths, looking for poachers' tracks, and keeping an alert eye on happenings in the bush. When linked by two-way radio to headquarters, such rangers can call for help when necessary, and if they vary their routine movements they can provide an unexpected and close surveillance in even the remotest corners of reserves. I have talked to several of the former game and park wardens who relied heavily on the use of men who knew how to track and move silently through the bush; consequently, they were able to provide exactly the sort of protection needed. Moreover, rangers in South Africa, who have been extremely successful in keeping poachers at bay, often claim that their successes are due to the African patrols on foot, bicycle and on horseback.

Since the early 1970s, however, Somali poachers in Kenya and Tanzania have had an almost free hand in some game areas, knowing that patrols are carried out almost exclusively by men in vehicles, which are noisy and give them plenty of lead time to slip into hiding. And vehicles are limited to moving around on roads, tracks and open areas.

The argument for more vehicles and air patrols runs along the lines that fewer men are needed and that a greater amount of territory can be covered in a shorter time; however, the fact remains that they can do no more than provide transport and a means of observation. Aircraft and vehicles should only be regarded as support materials for men on foot patrol who, admittedly, cost more to maintain than machines but are the only proven answer to the problem of safeguarding wildlife. Richard Bell and Ian Parker have studied the manpower requirements in Kenya and, although it is not possible to state the precise number of men needed to patrol every hundred square kilometres—because so much depends on such variables as the topography, the nature of the vegetation, and the pressure from people living along the boundaries—they estimate that around five times the present number of rangers need to be employed. However, Kenya is far from being the worst example of insufficient manpower in the field of wildlife conservation, and almost all parks and reserves in tropical Africa are vastly under-staffed, according to Parker's research. Yet, in all the countries with game areas in need of more rangers, there are serious problems due to unemployment. In Kenya there are only 1,000,000 paid jobs for a population of 16,000,000.

There is concern about the lack of sufficient rhino reproduction in the wild. In tandem with making their national parks safe for rhinos again, Kenya, Tanzania and Zambia are countries which could and should establish special breeding grounds for the black rhino. Such places could be set aside in existing parks and reserves, on private ranches or on sites unwanted elsewhere. It does not matter where they are located so long as they are suitable habitats for rhinos, completely surrounded by strong fences (preferably electrically charged), protected by border patrols and guarded day and night. The rhinos inside could be classified as national breeding herds and placed under the supervision of the appropriate government department in conjunction with a reputable international conservation organization willing to finance the project and to provide scientific expertise and equipment. The sole purpose of such breeding grounds would be to increase the numbers of black rhinos, so obviously no tourists or any other disturbances should be allowed which might affect the animals' well-being. This

Even the participation of the Kenya police with their modern equipment was insufficient to prevent poachers from killing many rhinos in the 1970s.

system would also make it possible for experts to study the behavioural patterns of rhinos in controlled surroundings and to follow up Dr John Goddard's work on the fertility rate of the females. We must learn the reasons for the decline in rhino pregnancies, which presently appear to occur every four years for the average female (Goddard estimated that the calving interval could be as frequent as every 27 months). We should try to discover what can be done to encourage higher reproductivity. My own view is that rhinos will breed quite normally again if they are kept in favourable conditions, maintained in good health and sheltered from man's harassment.

Until quite recently considerable numbers of rhinos lived on large tracts of land privately held by ranchers and farmers in upcountry Kenya. Much of this land is now being divided into smaller holdings for subsistence agriculture. Rhinos are unwelcome in these circumstances, so the Wildlife Conservation and Management Department has begun translocating some of the threatened rhinos both there and on the unprotected borders of Meru Park. Between March 1979 and August 1980 42 rhinos were captured; however, eight died shortly afterwards—a loss ratio that was high in comparison to an earlier translocation programme in Kenya carried out by John King in the mid 1960s, when only three out of 59 rhinos were lost. I am not aware of all the circumstances of the various capture attempts in the more recent translocation endeavours, but I do know that when eight rhinos were darted at Meru two of them died immediately. When two more were captured in the Aberdare mountains and later moved by lorry to Amboseli they were dumped to fend for themselves in a completely different type of environment with accordingly unfamiliar vegetation; both were dead within a few weeks—and their deaths were not caused by poachers.

In 1980, I visited the holding station for captured rhinos near Nyeri. I saw three rhinos in small, poorly constructed enclosures which had horizontal posts instead of vertical ones—horizontal posts are a danger to the rhinos' horns. The posts were held together with bits and pieces of wire, some of which had broken off thus constituting another menace to the rhinos. Whilst I was there, one of the men in charge chucked bundles of lucerne into the enclosures for the rhinos to eat, but the lucerne was soggy and damp and very tightly packed—hardly ideal feeding matter. What was even worse was the lack of sanitation in the enclosures. There was no way for them to drain properly, and the pathetic rhinos, which had been there for almost four months (while possible new homes for them were being discussed), had had to survive in a quagmire during the previous rains.

Certain members of the Department of Wildlife Conservation and Management have expressed dismay over the outcome of the translocation programme so far. Although most informed people believe that the concept is good, some experienced trappers say that there should have been better planning beforehand to prevent many of the catastrophes that have since arisen. For instance, according to Dr John King and John Seago, had the rhinos that were sent to Amboseli been given a chance for re-adjustment to their new environment by being kept in safe pens and slowly introduced to their new food, they would have probably been able to survive. Other conservationists have pointed out the importance of proper care for captured rhinos. If rhinos are to be held in enclosures before being translocated to areas where they will be expected to live as wild animals, then they should not be visited by crowds of people nor should they be kept in captivity any longer than absolutely necessary.

It is not easy to move rhinos around; but with skilled handling and proper management, successful translocation is possible. Nairobi Park obtained rhinos under these circumstances many years ago. There is also hope today that a breeding group of translocated rhinos can be established at Solio Ranch in Kenya, where the animals have 7,200 hectares of complete protection. A well-trained team of mounted guards on horseback patrols the boundary of the entire ranch from outside; another group of trained men daily checks the electric voltage on the two-and-a-half-metre high fence around the reserve; a lifetime of practical experience in game management enables the man in charge to provide sensible amenities for the wildlife, to keep regular counts of all the larger mammals, and to initiate changes necessary for their welfare. Individual rhinos are recognized on sight, thanks to a photographic record. The superbly cared for animals are a major asset to the country, and one of the shareholders of this ranch has been awarded the Order of the Golden Ark by Prince Bernhard of the Netherlands for this conservation achievement, which is paid for and managed by private funds.

In order to keep track of the additional 80 rhinos that Kenya's Wildlife Conservation and Management Department wants to translocate to national parks in the near future, a few officials advocate the use of radio collars. However, these are cumbersome and detract from the appearance of rhinos. One warden has discovered another possibility—drilling a small hole close to the base of the horn of a captured rhino and placing inside a tiny transistor bleeper which can be sealed up afterwards, leaving no obvious trace of its existence. As well as facilitating radio-tracking of rhinos on the move, transistors could also lead to the capture of poachers.

If poaching in East Africa is allowed to continue on its present scale, then serious thought will have to be given to the question of establishing a black rhino reserve on another continent where complete safety can be guaranteed. By moving Arabian oryx from the wild to Phoenix, Arizona, in 1962, wildlife enthusiasts were able to save that species from extinction in its natural desert habitat. By 1967 the oryx herd at Phoenix totalled 11 males and 6 females, comprising more than half of

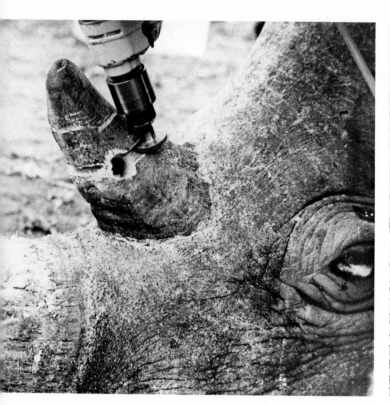

By drilling a groove around the horn, the antenna for a transistor can be held in place. Once the transistor and antenna are fitted, a scientist will follow the movements of this white rhino in South Africa.

the known world population of the animal. Now, a few of the Gulf States are making efforts to create new reserves in the former homeland of the oryx for some of the offspring of those that provided a breeding nucleus in the United States. It would be admitting defeat if African countries had to resort to a similar solution for black rhinos, and whilst I do not believe this species will become so endangered in the wild as the Arabian oryx, it may be advisable to make contingency plans for controlled breeding outside Africa. Black rhinos in ordinary zoos are reluctant to breed.

A hair-brained scheme to remove the horns of the rhinos in the wild has been suggested by more than one would-be conservationist. I cannot imagine how even half of the existing rhinos could be found, darted and have both their horns sawn off. Not only would this be a fantastically expensive operation, it would also have to be extremely thorough—and repeated at intervals since rhino horns do grow back. Moreover, after tracking a rhino for some time, what is there to keep a poacher from shooting the beast out of pure spite at the last moment when he discovers that its horn is missing? Besides, a rhino has various uses for its horns; some scientists contend that without them for defence cow rhinos would have difficulties in protecting their calves from predators. Moreover, fights among adult rhinos would be lethal if one were hornless.

Tourism geared to parks and reserves is more important to the conservation of wildlife in African countries than in Asia. The tourist industry earned Kenya about $180 million in 1981, and even those who spend the major part of their holiday on the coast choose Kenya because they can take excursions into game areas. Rhinos are amongst the top three animals that tourists want to see. Back in the 1950s and 1960s the long-horned rhinos of Amboseli were the main attraction of that reserve. I wonder if rhinos without horns would be all that popular? Nevertheless, a vociferous controversy over this totally impractical proposal raged for months in Nairobi in 1979. Henry Reuter, the managing editor of *Safari* magazine, summed it all up with the following comments:

If we are to start the nonsense of removing the horns of rhinos to save their lives,

123

why not extend the concept. We could, for example, de-tusk all the nation's elephants so as to make them less attractive to poachers. But we must not stop there, for poachers also seek the hairs of the elephant's tail for the making of bracelets ... We must remove the elephant's ears, because these are coveted as basic material for the making of boots and shoes. And while we are at it, we should perhaps remove a leg or two, because who knows when there will be a ready market for elephant foot umbrella stands?

But wait! Our vivisection campaign to save the wildlife is only just beginning. All the horns must of course be removed from the antelopes. The lions, leopards and cheetahs must be made to surrender their teeth and claws which are so much in demand by the modern jewellery trade, to say nothing of their skins ...

Just a few months before the famed naturalist and ornithologist Leslie Brown died in 1980, he proposed to a meeting of the African Rhino Group of the IUCN Survival Service Commission that both black and white rhinos be raised for commercial harvesting in South Africa. The main purpose of his idea was to produce various products for legitimate sale on the world market, under IUCN supervision. He thought that the supply would be ample enough to depress prices and to take some of the pressure off poaching for commercial gain. Leslie Brown was extremely pessimistic about the likelihood of African governments' stopping the illegal killing of rhinos, and offered this scheme as a possible means to meet the world demand for rhino horn and skin and conserve wild rhino populations at the same time. Regrettably, Dr Brown's paper was not discussed openly at the meeting, even though it contained many valid points. I think the main reason for this was that it is contrary to IUCN policy to encourage commercial trade in endangered species. Yet, there is also the question of whether or not Zimbabwe and South Africa will indefinitely hold on to their caches of rhino horn and not allow them onto international markets.

Among African governments there is a lack of co-operation in the prevention of wildlife smuggling from one country to another. If customs officers and police from neighbouring states were to work together on their border patrols and anti-smuggling intelligence operations, it would be a lot more difficult for dishonest traders to move rhino horn from one country to another. Furthermore, African countries without elephants or rhinos should also enforce restrictions on the trade. For example, Burundi is currently notorious for exporting ivory and rhino horn illegally taken from Zaire, Zambia, Tanzania, Uganda and Kenya. In early 1980 a government official issued a permit for the export of 37 tons of ivory, stating that this entire amount originated in Burundi (countries that are CITES signatories must receive with ivory imports documents from source countries confirming the legality of the sales). Nevertheless, there is not a single live elephant in all Burundi.

South Africa almost permanently lost the white rhinoceros at the end of the last century, but with the establishment of reserves in Natal in 1897, under proper management, the white rhino recovered. When the first scientific count was made in 1929 the population of the white rhino had increased to 150, and by 1960 the population stood at a healthy 645 animals. In the following year Natal Parks Board initiated a policy of translocating some of their white rhinos to other parks, reserves and zoos in South Africa and other countries of the world in order to re-stock the rhino in its former habitats in southern Africa and to fulfil the needs of zoos. From 1961 to August 1981, 2,566 white rhinos had been moved out of the Natal Parks, but despite this there are presently too many white rhinos in the Natal Parks. The vegetation in the last few years has been damaged very heavily by the white rhino, and even a record removal of 497 animals in the financial year 1980/1 has not rectified the problem. If new homes cannot be found for still many more white rhinos, then the authorities will have to consider cropping them in the next three to five years. In Kruger National Park, which had no white rhinos in 1961, there are now about 650; and the authorities there are already considering the possibility of having to kill some of them by the year 2000. From 1977 to 1981 the white rhinos in Kruger increased on average 10.1 per cent a year. There is simply now an embarrassment over the high number of white rhinos, and South Africa finds itself today in the unique position of having too many white rhinos. There are at present 2,500 of them in the various parks, reserves and on private ranches. A document prepared by the IUCN African Rhino Group in July 1980 states that the main problem of South African white rhinos is "overcrowding and insufficient places for translocation". The Natal Parks Board continues to look for ways of getting rid of surplus rhinos. It is presently charging only $735 each for sale to private Natal ranchers who wish to use white rhinos for breeding purposes, and $1,575 to ranchers who want to stock them for hunting safari clients. Overseas buyers may purchase rhinos for $2,100, plus crate ($580–$790) and transport charges. Despite the relatively low price for a potential zoo specimen, the market is not so great as might be expected. This is because the big expense is in getting the animal safely transported to its new home. In 1978 a respected international wildlife dealer charged $14,500 for guaranteed delivery of a white rhino in good health to any zoo in the world. In 1980, despite inflation and correspondingly higher transport costs, the dealer was offering to provide rhinos under the same conditions for $500 less. South African white rhinos are, in fact, now very much cheaper than black rhinos. In 1957 when several African countries were exporting live black rhinos, dealers sold them for $3,200, inclusive of delivery charges and a 30-day post-delivery insurance against death. The price went up to $10,000 in 1965, $17,500 in 1978 and $28,000 in 1980.

Purely from a commercial point of view, a white rhino is more valuable dead than alive when its skin and horn are sold to wholesalers in South-East Asia. Ian Parker and I have estimated that an adult white rhino can provide 120 kilos of dried hide worth $21,000 wholesale in Asia, and horns worth $1,800. In addition, its stomach, dried blood and other products could fetch another $1,500 at least. There would be some overhead expenses involved in drying and curing, but a clever businessman could make about $10,000 profit from the sale of the products of a single white rhino. I, of course, do not suggest that the Natal Parks Board should kill their surplus rhinos for the pharmaceutical trade; quite the contrary, I strongly urge a universal ban on the trade of rhino products (with the exception of urine and dung collected from live zoo specimens). A far better solution for surplus South African white rhinos would be to find new homes for them in other African countries such as Zimbabwe and Botswana which once had large rhino populations and which, with assistance from international conservation agencies, could provide the protection required for them.

I am also in favour of persuading some African governments to permit people to create and maintain private reserves for wildlife on the ranches that they own. Such reserves could become ideal sanctuaries for both black and white rhinos, paid for independently and run as private enterprises. Rather than conflicting with national parks, the private reserves could enhance the attraction of a country to wildlife enthusiasts, offering additional places to visit. Moreover, some might specialize in providing certain amenities unavailable to tourists in government-run parks. The managers of private wildlife reserves could experiment with new ideas to help conservation planning and encourage scientific studies of wild animals in controlled surroundings. Obviously, there would only be a very few ranchers in the position to afford to establish and run private game reserves in Africa, but I do not see why they should not be given encouragement to try to develop better management programmes.

Meanwhile, since there are too many white rhinos in Natal, the government has allowed some to be hunted in certain areas. There are now between 15 and 20 game ranches in Natal and another 10 in Transvaal where sportsmen, mainly North and South Americans, Spaniards and Italians, can shoot white rhinos and other game animals. From January to November 1981, they shot 12 white rhinos in Natal alone. Clients book a hunting trip for a minimum of 10 days; they pay $6,000 for a licence to hunt a rhino and about $300 a day for expenses in the bush. In all, it usually costs over $9,000 for such a safari. While shooting a white rhino is about as sporting as shooting a horse, this solution to the excess rhino population is gaining momentum in South Africa, which I understand is the only country in the world where rhinos can be legally hunted. It is ironic that South Africa has to dispose of its white rhinos this way when there is a great shortage of these most placid of all the rhino species elsewhere on the African continent.

If the existing rhino reserves in Africa and Asia could guarantee protection for the number of rhinos they are able to support, only the Javan rhino would still be the subject of concern. In order to help provide the safety necessary for rhinos an effort must be made to reduce the demand for rhino products in consumer countries. Until very recently, conservation agencies have given little thought to the matter of reducing demand. They have spent vast sums on vehicles and airplanes, on financing anti-poaching forces, on educational programmes, and on the creation of new parks and reserves. All this is imperative to combat poaching,

Samuel Ng'ethe, a Kenya Park Warden, gives domestic cow's milk mixed with glucose, vitamins and Farex to an orphaned black rhino calf.

but it does not stop people from buying rhino horn. So far wildlife organizations have effectively limited their attack on the trade to their efforts to encourage every country to ratify the CITES convention. Much more could be done.

North Yemen is the most prolific consumer of rhino horn and has no legislation to regulate its imports of this commodity; even if it did, how many people would obey the laws? Were CITES in effect, of course, it would be illegal for any rhino horn to enter the country; a certain amount of harassment could be directed at source countries that sent rhino horn to North Yemen, and the North Yemen government itself would be the subject of adverse publicity for allowing the ban on rhino imports to be ignored. None the less, CITES could not attack the root of the demand for the horn in North Yemen.

I think some other approaches might be worth trying. Since Yemenis are strict Muslims and have great respect for their Islamic *qadis*, someone should go to these leaders and explain the present slaughter of rhinos in Africa. There are strict hunting codes in the Koran, and more than one passage referring to animals ("No kind of beast is there on earth, nor fowl that flieth with its wings, but is a community like you"). Surely, the excessive killing of rhinos could be interpreted as inadvisable on religious grounds, and the leaders might consequently be willing to make some pronouncements against the use of rhino horn for dagger handles. At the same time, Yemeni merchants should be approached and asked to determine what substitutes would be acceptable as valuable alternatives to rhino horn and how the Yemenis could be persuaded to use them instead for their dagger handles.

An idea put forth by many conservationists to depress the prices for rhino horn—and thus discourage poaching—is to flood the market with artificial horn. This will not work. People have already tried to substitute walrus and wart-hog ivory for that of elephant, and even though it is natural-looking, people do not want either in place of what comes from "Jumbo". There have also been large-scale attempts at producing artificial ivory carvings, with factories turning out netsukes, statues and jewellery made from innumerable synthetics looking almost identical to ivory pieces. Yet the price of real ivory increased ten-fold in the 1970s. I visited a factory that produces fake elephant ivory carvings, the Lung Da Arts Company in Taipei. It advertises its products in trade magazines and to the public in the following manner:

> Not all ivory comes from elephants. The cruel slaughter of large numbers of elephants in Africa and other areas in the world, to supply the "ivory trade", is one of the disgraces of our times. And it is all so unnecessary. You can buy imitation ivory products from Lung Da that only an expert can distinguish from the real thing.

Although the prices for Lung Da netsukes and figurines are less than a tenth of what they would cost if they were carved out of elephant ivory, they are not in very high demand. In fact, I was asked if I could find a market for them in Kenya!

Most rhino horn is sold for pharmaceutical uses. As noted earlier, wholesalers will not usually handle rhinoceros horn shavings because they are wary of their authenticity. So whole horns would have to be manufactured out of synthetics—and that would be extremely difficult. Each horn would have to be individualized and would also have to be capable of withstanding the same processing that real rhino horn undergoes. The fact is that wholesalers would not touch whole rhino horns unless they were convinced they were genuine—they know that their reputations would be ruined if they tried to sell fakes to those who prescribe horn as a medicine. If dealers in artificial horn tried to bypass the traders by going directly to the retail shops, the pharmacists would immediately become suspicious and contact the wholesalers and make enquiries about the alleged source. They would not want to try to trick their customers. Furthermore, just as soon as traders, retailers and customers knew that there was artificial rhino horn being sold, they would blame the conservationists for this development. Conservation organizations would lose their credibility, and traders in South-East Asia and the Far East would be all the more reluctant to co-operate with them in the future to conserve endangered species.

In 1980 some people in Tanzania did attempt to fake rhino horn. In Shinyanga in the northern part of the country, several swindlers started a business of lining ordinary cow horns with metal and then coating them with plastic to simulate the appearance of real rhino horn. They sold them as authentic rhino horns for the equivalent of $875 a kilo. According to the Shinyanga Regional Crimes Officer, some of the swindlers were later found murdered.

There are more effective ways of decreasing rhino horn sales than by trying to deceive people. I think that many traders would listen to co-ordinated pleas made to them by straightforward conservationists. There are probably no more than a hundred wholesale traders directly importing rhino horn; and, to my knowledge, not one of them deals exclusively in that commodity. Moreover, the traders in Hong Kong have voluntarily stopped purchasing rhino horn from abroad, and the reasons for their decision to stop doing so are also valid for traders in other countries. Since rhino horn is only one of literally hundreds of products handled by traditional pharmacists, there would be little economic hardship caused to them by foregoing rhino horn sales.

I do not think it is possible to try to convince traditional Chinese doctors that rhino horn lacks the qualities they ascribe to it, nor should one try to prove this to them. Several people have said that a rumour should be spread to the effect that rhino horn is carcinogenic or that African rhinos are suffering from some newly discovered disease that affects their horns. Again, these are arguments designed to trick buyers and would be seen as such.

In many parts of Asia, the Chinese practitioners of traditional medicine belong to professional associations. The heads of these organizations should be approached and asked to dissuade their members from prescribing rhino products because the demand is too great for the supply, and rhinos are consequently endangered. I have already talked to some doctors who have said that they would be willing to prescribe saiga antelope horns as a substitute. Since these animals are commercially harvested for sale under controlled conditions, this would not threaten their survival.

Although conservationists may rejoice in the fact that Japan ratified CITES in November 1980 without making an exemption for rhino horn imports, I do not think they should consider that the end of the matter. The Japanese have traditionally used rhino horn for even the most common of afflictions—the cold. What are they going to do when present stocks run out? Are the traders going to abide strictly by the law when there remains a strong demand for this product, knowing that people elsewhere are still legally selling it? Rhino horn can be cut into small pieces without lessening its value, and it is not easy for customs officials to detect it then. The situation is such that it could be tempting to some, not necessarily wholesale importers, but quite possibly homeward-bound Japanese tourists, to buy supplies in other countries. When I was studying the rhino trade in Japan in November 1980, I was astounded that I could not find a single person (aside from those belonging to conservation agencies) who knew anything about the plight of the rhino.

It would not be at all difficult to run a campaign to educate the Japanese in conservation measures that must be taken to try to save rhinos. In Japan, as in England, there are national newspapers which have millions of readers. Articles should be written for them, pointing out the rhino problem, teaching why it is necessary to protect the remaining populations, and captivating readers by making these articles factual, poignant and of direct interest. Such a campaign would be addressed to adults; but children, too, should be made aware of the situation. Stories for them, composed by respected Japanese authors of children's literature, could be commissioned. I think that Japanese children, like those elsewhere, generally have to be persuaded to take any medicine, and if they are attracted to the idea that rhinos are rather special creatures that deserve care in the wild, they are going to be even more reluctant to consume something that is only available as a result of such an animal being killed.

Most likely, further studies on wildlife will reveal greater possibilities for world-wide conservation measures and the control of trade in endangered species.

My own story of the rhinos is told with the hope that governments, conservation agencies and wildlife dealers will come to realize the importance of working together to save these animals.

Rufus sometimes walked up the front steps of the Sheldricks' verandah and poked his head through the sitting-room window, looking for the Sheldricks' daughter, Angela, who was one of his best friends.

Bibliography

African Rhino Group. *Newsletter*, No. 1 (April 1980).

Anderson, Charles John. *Lake Ngami; or, Explorations and Discoveries During Four Years Wanderings in the Wilds of South Western Africa*. London: Hurst and Blackett, 1856.

Ansell, W.F.H. "The Black Rhinoceros in Zambia", *Oryx*, Vol. 10, No. 3 (December 1969), pp. 176–92.

Ansorge, W.J. *Under the African Sun: A Description of Native Races in Uganda, Sporting Adventures and Other Experiences*. London: William Heinemann, 1899.

Axelson, Eric. *South East Africa 1488–1530*. London: Longman, Green, 1940.

———. *Portuguese in South-East Africa: 1600–1700*. Johannesburg: Witwatersrand University Press, 1964.

Baker, Sir Samuel W. *The Nile Tributaries of Abyssinia and the Sword Hunters of the Hamran Arabs*. London: Macmillan, 1867.

———. *Wild Beasts and Their Ways: Reminiscences of Europe, Asia, Africa and America*. London: Macmillan, 1890.

Balfour, Edward. *Encyclopaedia Asiatica: Comprising Indian Subcontinent, Eastern and Southern Asia, Commercial, Industrial and Scientific*. Vol. 8. New Delhi: Cosmos Publications (reprint), 1976.

Beveridge, Annette Susannah, editor and translator. *Babur-Nama (Memoirs of Babur)*. New Delhi: Oriental Books Reprint Corporation (reprint), March 1970.

Boonsong Lekagul and McNeely, Jeffrey A. *Mammals of Thailand*. Bangkok: Association for the Conservation of Wildlife, 1977.

Borges, Jorge Luis. *The Book of Imaginary Beings*. London: Jonathan Cape, 1970.

Boudet, Jacques. *Man and Beast: A Visual History*. New York: Golden Press, 1964.

Brocklehurst, Capt. H.C. *Game Animals of the Sudan: Their Habits and Distribution*. London: Gurney and Jackson, 1931.

Brown, William Harvey. *On the South African Frontier: The Adventures and Observations of an American in Mashonaland and Matabeleland*. London: Sampson Low, Marston, 1899.

Burchell, William J. *Travels in the Interior of Southern Africa*. Two vols. London: Batchworth Press, 1953 (original: 1822–4).

Burton, Richard F. *The Lake Regions of Central Africa; A Picture of Exploration*. Two vols. London: Longman, 1860.

Carter, Nick. *The Arm'd Rhinoceros*. London: Andre Deutsch, 1965.

China, Republic of. Chinese Maritime Customs, Statistical Department. *The Trade of China, 1966–1978*. Taipei: Inspectorate General of Customs, 1967–79.

Chinese Medical Dictionary. Vol. 2 [in Mandarin]. Hong Kong: 1978.

Cobb, Steve. "The Rhino's Last Trump". *Wildlife News*, Vol. 14, No 2 (1979), pp. 10–12.

Cott, Hugh B. *Looking at Animals: A Zoologist in Africa*. London: Collins, 1975.

Cowie, Col. Mervyn. *Fly, Vulture*. London: George G. Harrap, 1961.

———. "Here's How It All Began", *Africana*, Vol. 2, No. 7 (March 1966), p. 6.

Daly, Marcus. *Big Game Hunting and Adventure: 1897–1936*. London: Macmillan, 1937.

Davey, Neil. "Wildlife in Miniature", *Wildlife*, Vol. 21, No. 10 (October 1979), pp. 36–7.

Denis, Armand. *On Safari: The Story of My Life*. London: Companion Book Club, 1964.

Douglas-Hamilton, I., Hillman, A.K.K., Holt, P., and Ansell, P. "Luangwa Valley: Elephant, Rhino and Wildlife Survey". Nairobi, October 1979. (Mimeographed.)

Duyvendak, J.J.L. *China's Discovery of Africa*. London: Arthur Probsthain, 1949.

East African Customs and Excise Department. *Annual Trade Reports of Tanganyika, Uganda and Kenya 1970–1976*. Mombasa: various years.

Feinberg, Lawrence. *Catalogue Five: Rare and Important Books and Manuscripts*. Brooklyn: Lawrence Feinberg, 1980.

Fisher, James, Simon, Noel, and Vincent, Jack. *The Red Book: Wildlife in Danger*. London: Collins, 1964.

Foa, Edouard. *Résultats scientifiques des Voyages d'Edouard Foa*. Paris: Imprimerie nationale, 1908.

Gee, E.P. *The Wild Life of India*. London: Collins, 1964.

Goddard, John, "Aerial Census of Black Rhinoceros Using Stratified Random Sampling", *East African Wildlife Journal*, Vol. 7 (August 1969), pp. 105–14.

Guggisberg, C.A.W. *S.O.S. Rhino*. Nairobi: East African Publishing House, 1966.

Halliday, Fred. *Arabia Without Sultans*. Harmondsworth: Penguin Books, 1974.

Hamilton, P.H., and King, J.M. "The Fate of Black Rhinoceroses Released in Nairobi National Park", *East African Wildlife Journal*, Vol. 7 (August 1969), pp. 73–83.

Harrison, Tom. "Rhinoceros in Borneo: and Traded to China", *Sarawak Museum Journal*, Vol. 7, No. 8 New Series, No. 23 Old Series (1956), pp. 259–74.

Hillman, Kes. "Trying to Save the Rhino", *Swara*, Vol. 2, No. 3 (May-June 1979), pp. 22–7.

Hirth, Friedrich, and Rockhill, W.W. *Chau Ju-Kua: His Work on the Chinese and Arab Trade in the Twelfth and Thirteenth Centuries, Entitled Chu-fan-Chi*. Amsterdam: Oriental Press, 1966.

Ho Peng-Yoke. "Traditional Chinese Medicine up to Date", *Hemisphere*, Vol. 23, No. 4 (July-August 1979), pp. 250–6.

Holman, Dennis. *The Elephant People*. London: John Murray, 1967.

Hubback, Theodore. "The Two-Horned Asiatic Rhinoceros (*Dicerorhinus*)", *Journal of the Bombay Natural History Society*, Vol. 40, No. 4 (May 1939), pp. 594–617.

Hunter, J.A. *Hunter*. London: Hamish Hamilton, 1952.

al-Idrisi. *India and the Neighbouring Territories*, edited and translated by S. Maqbul Ahmad. Leiden: E.J. Brill, 1960.

India, Government of. *The Wild Life (Protection) Act, 1972*. Delhi: Controller of Publications, 1974.

———. Imperial Gazetteer. Provincial Series. *Burma*. Vol. 1. Calcutta: Superintendent of Government Printing, 1908.

Ingrams, W.H. *Zanzibar: Its History and Its People*. London: H.F. & G. Witherby, 1931.

Institute of Developing Economies, Tokyo. *Foreign Trade Statistics of Japan, 1951–1965. Time Series by Commodity*. Vol. 1: *Table of Commodity Totals in Time Series*. Tokyo: I.D.E., 1972.

———. *Foreign Trade Statistics of Thailand, 1950–1969. Time Series by Commodity*. Vol. I. Tokyo: I.D.E., 1974.

Japan, Government of. *Japan: Exports and Imports; Commodity by Country, 1966–1978*. Tokyo: Ministry of Finance, 1967–79.

Jenyns, Soame. "The Chinese Rhinoceros and Chinese Carvings in Rhinoceros Horn", *Transactions of the Oriental Ceramic Society 1954–1955* (1957), pp. 31–61.

Kaweche, G.B., and Mwenye, A.N. "Recreation Hunting in Zambia." Paper for the Fifth Regional Wildlife Conference for East and Central Africa. Gaberone, Botswana, July 1978. (Mimeographed.)

Kearney, Yuilleen. *Rufus the Rhino*. London: Collins, 1965.

Keller, W. Phillip. *Africa's Wild Glory*. London: Jarrolds Publishers, 1959.

Kenya, Government of. *Annual Trade Reports of the Kenya Customs and Excise Department 1977 and 1978*. Mombasa: 1978 and 1979.

Keys, John D. *Chinese Herbs: Their Botany, Chemistry and Pharmacodynamics*. Rutland, Vermont: Charles E. Tuttle (no date).

King, J.M. "The Capture and Translocation of the Black Rhinoceros", *East African Wildlife Journal*, Vol. 7 (August 1969), pp. 115–130.

Kingdon, Jonathan. *East African Mammals: An Atlas of Evolution in Africa*. Vol. 3, Part B: *Large Mammals*. London: Academic Press, 1979.

Kipling, John Lockwood. *Beast and Man in India: A Popular Sketch of Indian Animals in Their Relations with the People*. London: Macmillan, 1891.

Kirkman, James. *Men and Monuments on the East African Coast*. London: Lutterworth Press, 1964.

Kittenberger, Kalman. *Big Game Hunting and Collecting in East Africa 1903–1926*. London: Edward Arnold, 1929.

Korea, Republic of. *Statistical Yearbook of Foreign Trade 1970–1978*. Seoul: Office of Customs Administration, 1971–9.

Kunz, F. *Ivory and the Elephant in Arts, Archaeology and Science*. New York: Doubleday, 1916.

Kunzang, Ven Renchung Rinpoche Jampal. *Tibetan Medicine*. Berkeley and Los Angeles: University of California Press, 1976.

Lahan, P., and Sonowal, R.N. "Kaziranga Wild Life Sanctuary, Assam", *Journal of the Bombay Natural History Society*, Vol. 70, No. 2 (August 1973), pp. 245–78.

Laurie, William Andrew, "The Ecology and Behaviour of the Greater One-Horned Rhinoceros". Unpublished Ph.D. dissertation, University of Cambridge, December 1978.

Laws, R.M., Parker, I.S.C., and Johnstone, R.C.B. *Elephants and Their Habitats*. Oxford: Clarendon Press, 1975.

Leakey, Louis S.B. *The Wild Realm: Animals of East Africa*. Washington, D.C.: National Geographic Society, 1969.

Levron, Jacques. *Daily Life at Versailles in the Seventeenth and Eighteenth Centuries*. London: George Allen and Unwin, 1968.

Lydekker, R. *The Game Animals of Africa*. London: Rowland Ward, 1908.

Lyell, D.D. *Hunting Trips in Northern Rhodesia*. London: Horace Cox, 1910.

McCutcheon, John T. *In Africa: Hunting Adventures in the Big Game Country*. Indianapolis: Bobbs-Merrill, 1910.

McNeely, J.A. "Is There a Future for Thai Forests?", *Conservation News*, September 1977, pp. 1–5.

McNeely, Jeffrey A., and Cronin, Edward W. "Rhinos in Thailand", *Oryx*, Vol. 11, No. 6 (September 1972), pp. 457–60.

MacQueen, Peter. *In Wildest Africa*. Boston: L.C. Page, 1909.

Martin, Esmond Bradley. *Zanzibar: Tradition and Revolution*. London: Hamish Hamilton, 1978.

———. "The Geography of Present-Day Smuggling in the Western Indian Ocean", *The Great Circle: Journal of the Australian Association for Maritime History*, Vol. 1, No. 2 (October 1979), pp. 18–35.

———. *The International Trade in Rhinoceros Products*. Gland, Switzerland: International Union for Conservation of Nature and Natural Resources and

World Wildlife Fund, 1980.

———. "The Rhino: Grim Prospects for Survival", *Africana*, Vol. 7, No. 2 (April 1980), pp. 15, 16 and 19.

———. "The Conspicuous Consumption of Rhinos", *Animal Kingdom*, Vol. 84, No. 1 (February–March 1981), pp. 10–19, and Vol. 84, No. 2 (April–May 1981), pp. 20–9.

———. "India's Rhino Horn Trade", *Africana*, Vol. 8, No. 1 (April 1981), p. 31.

Martin, Esmond Bradley, and Hillman, Kes. "The State of the Game: Death Knell for the Rhino", *Safari* (April–May 1979), p. 5.

———. "Count-down for Rhino in Kenya", *Africana*, Vol. 6, No. 12 (3rd quarter 1979), pp. 5–6.

———. "Will Poaching Exterminate Kenya's Rhino?", *Oryx*, Vol. 15, No. 2 (November 1979), pp. 131–2.

Martin, Esmond Bradley, and Martin, Chryssee Perry. *Cargoes of the East: The Ports, Trade and Culture of the Arabian Seas and Western Indian Ocean*. London: Elm Tree Books/Hamish Hamilton, 1978.

Martin, Esmond Bradley, and Parker, I.S.C. "Trade in African Rhino Horn", *Oryx*, Vol. 15, No. 2 (November 1979), pp. 153–8.

———. "Exploding Some of the Myths about Rhino Horns", *Africana*, Vol. 7, No. 3 (December 1980), pp. 12–13.

Mills, J.V.G., editor. *Ma Huan. Ying-Yai Sheng-Lan: The Overall Survey of the Ocean's Shores [1433]*. Cambridge: Hakluyt Society, 1970.

Moseley, Ray. "Of Rhinos, Elephants, Poachers and War", *Chicago Tribune Magazine*, 16 March 1980, pp. 16–24.

Moss, Cynthia. *Portraits in the Wild: Animal Behaviour in East Africa*. London: Hamish Hamilton, 1976.

Mulder, Monique Borgerhoff, and Caro, Tim. "Slaughter of the Elephants", *New Scientist*, 3 July 1980, pp. 32–4.

Nachtigal, Gustav. *Sahara and Sudan*. Vol. 1: *Tripoli and Fezzan, Tibesti or Tu*. London: Hurst, 1974.

Nadkarni, Dr. K.M. *Indian Materia Medica: With Ayurvedic, Unani-Tibbi, Siddha, Allopathic, Homeopathic, Naturopathic and Home Remedies*. Two vols. Bombay: Popular Prakas, 1976.

Needham, Joseph. *Science and Civilization in China*. Vol. 4: *Physics and Physical Technology*. Cambridge: Cambridge University Press, 1971.

Nicholls, C.S. *The Swahili Coast: Politics, Diplomacy and Trade on the East African Littoral: 1798–1856*. London: George Allen & Unwin, 1971.

Nripendra, Narayana Bhupa, Maharaja of Cooch Behar. *Thirty-Seven Years of Big Game Hunting in Cooch Behar, the Duars and Assam*. London: Bennett, Coleman, 1908.

Owen-Smith, Rupert Norman. "The Behavioural Ecology of the White Rhinoceros". Unpublished Ph.D. dissertation, University of Wisconsin, 1973.

Pankhurst, Richard. *Economic History of Ethiopia 1800–1935*. Addis Ababa: Haile Selassie I University Press, 1968.

Pant, G.N. *Indian Arms and Armour*. Two vols. New Delhi: Army Educational Stores, January 1978 and January 1980.

Parker, I.S.C. "The Ivory Trade". Report for the U.S. Fish and Wildlife Service. Nairobi, 1979. (Mimeographed.)

Pitman, Captain C.R.S. *A Game Warden Among his Charges*. London: Nisbet, 1931.

Pollok, F.T., *Sport in British Burmah, Assam and the Cassyah and Jyntiah Hills*. Two vols. London: Chapman and Hall, 1879.

———. *Incidents of Foreign Sport and Travel*. London: Chapman and Hall, 1894.

Pollok, F.T., and Thom, W.S. *Wild Sports of Burma and Assam*. London: Hurst and Blackett, 1900.

Polo, Marco. *The Book of Ser Marco Polo, the Venetian, Concerning the Kingdoms and Marvels of the East*. The Yule Edition. New York: Airmont, 1969.

Prater, S.H. *The Book of Indian Animals*. 3rd ed., revised. Bombay: Bombay Natural History Society, 1971.

Read, Bernard E. *Chinese Materia Medica: Animal Drugs*. Taipei: Southern Materials Center, 1976.

Reuter, Henry J. "Saving the Animals" (editorial), *Safari*, June–July 1979, p. 3.

Ripley, S. Dillon. *The Land and Wildlife of Tropical Asia*. Netherlands: Time-Life International, 1965.

Ritchie, A.T.A. "The Black Rhinoceros (*Diceros bicornis*)", *East African Wildlife Journal*, Vol. 1 (August 1963), pp. 54–62.

Robinson, Harry. *Monsoon Asia: A Geographical Survey*. New York: Praeger Publications, 1967.

Rookmaaker, L.C. "Rhinoceros and Man in Borneo", *Sarawak Museum Journal*, Vol. 24, No. 45 New Series (1976), pp. 293–8.

Roth, H.H. "White and Black Rhinoceros in Rhodesia", *Oryx*, Vol. 9, No. 3 (1967), pp. 217–31.

Rowland, Beryl. *Animals with Human Faces: A Guide to Animal Symbolism*. London: George Allen & Unwin, 1974.

"Saving Asia's Wild Treasures", *Asiaweek*, Vol. 5, No. 37 (21 September 1979), pp. 26–31.

Schenkel, R., and Schenkel, L. "General Report and Synopsis of SSC Asian Rhino Specialist Group, Special Meeting". Bangkok, 13–16 August 1979. (Mimeographed.)

Selous, Frederick Courtney. *African Nature Notes and Reminiscenses*. London: Macmillan, 1908.

Seshadri, Balakrishna. *The Twilight of India's Wildlife*. London: John Baker, 1969.

Sheldrick, Daphne. *The Orphans of Tsavo*. London: Collins and Harvill Press, 1966.

———. *The Tsavo Story*. London: Collins and Harvill Press, 1973.

Simon, Noel. *Between the Sunlight and the Thunder: The*

Wildlife of Kenya. Boston: Houghton Mifflin, 1963.

Spillett, J. Juan. "A Report on Wild Life Surveys in North India and Southern Nepal, January-June 1966", *Journal of the Bombay Natural History Society,* Vol. 63, No. 3 (1967), pp. 492–628.

Stelfox, John, and Kufwafwa, John. "Distributions, Densities and Trends of Elephants and Rhinoceros in Kenya, 1977–78, from Kenya Rangeland Ecological Monitoring Unit Aerial Surveys". Nairobi, 30 April 1979. (Mimeographed.)

Sutherland, Robert. *Zambesi Camp Fires.* London: H.F. & G. Witherby, 1935.

Tabler, Edward C. *The Far Interior: Chronicles of Pioneering in the Matabele and Mashona Countries, 1847–1879.* Capetown: A.A. Balkema, 1955.

Taiwan. National Palace Museum, Taipei. *Masterpieces of Chinese Miniature Crafts in the National Palace Museum.* Taipei: National Palace Museum, 1976.

Talbot, Lee Merriam. "A Look at Threatened Species", *Oryx,* Vol. 5 (May 1960), pp. 153–293.

Tatton, Lord Egerton of. *Indian and Oriental Armour.* London: Arms and Armour Press, 1968.

Thailand, Government of. *Foreign Trade Statistics of Thailand.* Bangkok: Department of Customs, various years.

Thomas, Thomas Morgan. *Eleven Years in Central South Africa.* Bulawayo: Rhodesian Reprint Library, 1970 (original: 1873).

Traditional Chinese Medicine: Herbal, Mineral and Organic: An Exhibition Sponsored by the National Museum and the Institute of Chinese Medical Studies, Singapore. Singapore: 1979.

Uganda, Government of. *Annual Reports of the Game Department of the Uganda Protectorate 1936–1948.* Entebbe: Government Printer, various years.

Uganda, Tanganyika and Kenya, Governments of. *Blue Books, 1926–1948.*

"Uganda's Elephants Face Extinction", *IUCN Bulletin,* New Series, Vol. 2, No. 4 (April 1980), p.1.

Wallnofer, Heinrich, and Rottauscher, Anna von. *Chinese Folk Medicine.* New York: New American Library, 1972.

Watt, George. *A Dictionary of the Economic Products of India.* Vol. 6, Part 1. Calcutta: Office of the Superintendent of Government Printing, 1892.

———. *Indian Art at Delhi 1903.* London: John Murray, 1904.

Wheatley, Paul. "The Land of Zanj: Exegetical Notes on Chinese Knowledge of East Africa Prior to A.D. 1500", in Steel, Robert W., and Prothero, R. Mansell, *Geographers and the Tropics: Liverpool Essays.* London: Longman, 1964.

Wheatley, Paul. "Analecta Sino-Africana Recensa", in Chittick, Neville, and Rotberg, Robert I., editors, *East Africa and the Orient: Cultural Syntheses in Pre-Colonial Times.* New York: Africana Publishing Company, 1975.

World Bank. *Yemen Arab Republic: Development of a Traditional Economy.* Washington, D.C.: World Bank, 1979.

World Wildlife Fund. *Yearbooks, 1965–1967, 1968, 1969, 1970/71–1979/80.*

———. *Monthly Reports,* various months and years.

Yemen Arab Republic, Central Bank of Yemen. *Annual Reports, 1969/70–1976/7.* Sanaa: Central Bank of Yemen, various years.

Picture Credits

All photographs by *Mohamed Amin*, except the following:

Index